COLOSSIANS AND PHILEMON

Colossians and Philemon

The Supremacy of Christ

Wendell K. Grout

CHRISTIAN PUBLICATIONS, INC.
CAMP HILL, PENNSYLVANIA

Christian Publications, Inc.
3825 Hartzdale Drive, Camp Hill, PA 17011
www.cpi-horizon.com
www.christianpublications.com

Faithful, biblical publishing since 1883

Colossians and Philemon
ISBN: 0-87509-628-X

LOC Control Number: 00-135130

© 2001 by Christian Publications, Inc.

Printed in the United States of America

01 02 03 04 05   5 4 3 2 1

Contents

*Part 2: The Sanctification and
Service of the People of Christ
(Practical)*

Philemon

Introduction

Our pulpit studies take us to Paul's epistle to the Colossians, where the theme is "The Supremacy and Sufficiency of Christ." Most scholars agree that in none of his other writings does Paul reach the heights of Christology that he does in this four-chapter letter. It is profoundly Christ-focused.

Colosse was a rather small city at the time of this writing. It was located about 100 miles east of the city of Ephesus in the country that is now Turkey. It was somewhat overshadowed by the larger nearby centers of Laodicea and Hierapolis.

Paul never visited Colosse. In all probability, the pastor of the church had been Epaphras. We believe that he had been converted through the apostle's ministry in Ephesus, later entered into missionary work and went to Colosse, preaching the gospel. People responded in faith and a church was formed (Colossians 4:12-13).

At the time of the writing, Epaphras was in Rome in prison with Paul (Philemon 23). He had gone with information about the church. Most of what was reported was evidently very favorable, but there were some concerns shared regarding some teaching coming into the church that detracted from the person and work of Christ.

This doctrine seemed to center on a false legalism, a false asceticism and a false mysticism. In the first, some were teaching that the observance of certain sacred days and seasons, along with various rituals, were essential to the full Christian experience. In the second, others were teaching that the highest spiritual plain was reached by practicing severe bodily austerities. The congregation must follow extreme regulations in regard to natural appetites. In the third, the teaching emphasized the need for special revelation through visions and dreams. The worship of angels was also a part of this very esoteric and professedly elevated group.

To counteract and correct these heresies, the inspired apostle shows the absolute supremacy and sufficiency of Christ. One of the key verses says it so well, "For in Christ all the fullness of the Deity lives in bodily form, and you have been given fullness in Christ, who is the head over every power and authority" (Colossians 2:9-10).

This letter addresses the ongoing problem that we all have naturally—to add things to the Lord Jesus and His work, making them essential to our salvation and sanctification. Someone has pointed out that when we do this, what we add soon gets more attention and takes on more importance than the Lord Himself. These "distinctives" then become the standard by which we judge all spiritual experience.

Colossians divides quite simply in the following way:

1. The Supremacy and Sufficiency of the Person of Christ. Chapters 1-2 (Theological)
2. The Sanctification and Service of the People of Christ. Chapters 3-4 (Practical)

A final chapter in this commentary will be devoted to a study of the brief epistle of Philemon. Philemon was a wealthy member of the Colossian assembly. One of his slaves, Onesimus, had run away and gone to Rome. In some mysterious way, by God's providence, he had come into contact with Paul in prison and was gloriously converted. Paul was sending him back to his master with the letter to explain what had happened and to appeal to Philemon's highest Christian character in dealing with his runaway slave who was now his brother in Christ.

Onesimus was to accompany Tychicus, a close associate of Paul, who had been charged by the apostle to carry the Colossian epistle, inform the congregation of Paul's condition and then encourage the saints (Colossians 4:7-9).

So the two letters are closely related. In Colossians we have a major statement regarding the preeminence and sufficiency of Christ, and in Philemon we see how knowing and experiencing this wonderful Person works itself out in practical ways in the social and cultural patterns of a pagan world.

Part 1

The Supremacy and Sufficiency of the Person of Christ

(Theological)

Christis:
The Focus of Our Faith

Colossians 1:1-8

Paul, an apostle of Christ Jesus by the will of God, and Timothy our brother,
To the holy and faithful brothers in Christ at Colosse:
Grace and peace to you from God our Father.
We always thank God, the Father of our Lord Jesus Christ, when we pray for you, because we have heard of your faith in Christ Jesus and of the love you have for all the saints—the faith and love that spring from the hope that is stored up for you in heaven and that you have already heard about in the word of truth, the gospel that has come to you. All over the world this gospel is bearing fruit and growing, just as it has been doing among you since the day you heard it and understood God's grace in all its truth. You learned it from Epaphras, our dear fellow servant, who is a faithful minister of Christ on our behalf, and who also told us of your love in the Spirit.

Christ is the focus of our faith. Paul was writing to people who had placed their faith in Jesus Christ. This wasn't just intellectual assent to a theological position. This was moral consent and spiritual commitment to a living, vital Person. These people knew Christ and had placed their faith in him. Colossians 1:4 says, "because we have heard of your faith in Christ Jesus" and the same thing is repeated in a different way in 2:5: "For though I am absent from you in body, I am present with you in spirit and delight to see how orderly you are and how firm your faith in Christ is." My question to all of us is this—have we placed our personal faith in Jesus Christ? This epistle will help us to answer that question.

We are just looking at the salutation and the introduction to the letter. We don't have any profound theology here, but even in the greeting that Paul gave to these saints in Colosse, he said a lot about what it means to place our faith in Christ. Several things take place when we do that.

Faith in Christ Brings Us into a Spiritual Brotherhood (1:1-2)

We are brought into a spiritual fraternity when we place our faith in the Lord Jesus. "Paul, an apostle of Jesus Christ by the will of God, and Timothy our brother, To the holy and faithful brothers in Christ at Colosse" (1:1-2). Other Scriptures which speak about this brotherhood are found in 4:7, 9 and 15.

True brotherhood is not found in fraternal orders, political parties, social gatherings, military units, ethnic groupings, professional societies or sports teams, but rather in Christ. Our brotherhood in the Christian faith is to be found in a Person. When we placed our faith in the Lord Jesus we came into Christ and a wonderful spiritual fraternity.

Our brotherhood is found in a Person but it functions in a place. It is important for us to see that all believers have a position *and* a location. What we are in our position should be seen in how we function in our location. Paul speaks to "the holy and faithful brothers in Christ at Colosse." They were special people to whom Paul wrote, special because they were in Christ. In this pagan community of Colosse they were community within the community. They were a brotherhood within the social structure of their city.

My church and I are a brotherhood in our city of Calgary. We are in Christ—that's our position—but we live in Calgary—that's our location. In our location we should demonstrate that we are in Christ. We should show forth the fact that we are vitally related to Jesus Christ, that it is in Him that we live and move and have our being. We are rooted and grounded in Him. We find in Him our life, our sustenance, our strength, our joy. All that we require in time and eternity, life here and life there, is found in this wonderful Person. We are going to see more about that as we get into the letter.

Our position in Christ is essential, our location incidental. It doesn't really matter where you live. Paul was writing from a prison cell with a chain on his wrist, but he was in Christ. When he wrote to the Philippians, did he say, "Rejoice in your circumstances"? No. "Rejoice in your position?" No. "Rejoice in your possessions?" No. "Rejoice in your surroundings?" No. What did he say? "Rejoice in the Lord." Paul had learned the secret of being in Christ even when he was held in prison. Whatever our circumstances are, however difficult we may find our environment, if we are in Christ we can rise above it. We can bloom where we are planted. We can thrive and flourish in whatever the environment may be. Let me quote from Barclay:

> A Christian always moves in two spheres. He is in a certain place in this world, but he is also in Christ. He lives in two dimensions. He lives in this world whose duties he does not treat lightly. But above and beyond that, he lives in Christ. In this world he may move

from place to place but wherever he is he is in Christ. That is why outward circumstances make little difference to the Christian. His peace and his joy are not dependent on them. That is why he will do any job with all his heart. It may be menial, unpleasant, painful. It may be far less distinguished than he might expect to have. Its rewards may be small and its praise nonexistent; nevertheless, the Christian will do it diligently, uncomplainingly, and cheerfully, for he is in Christ and does all things as to the Lord. We are all in our own Colosse but we are all in Christ and it is Christ who sets the tone of our living.[1]

When I am in Christ it should make a difference in the boardroom. It should make a difference in the office, in the school, in my home. When I am in Christ it should make a difference in the crises of life. It should make a difference when temptation comes, when trials flood over my soul, when dark and difficult days dawn upon me. If I am in Christ, I have all that I need. All the vital resources for the Christian life are found in this glorious Person. Are you in Christ today? I hope you are.

Faith in Christ Makes Us Holy People (1:2)

And then faith in Christ makes us holy people. Notice that 1:2 says, "To the *holy* and faithful brothers in Christ at Colosse" (emphasis mine). The King James Version translates this "saints." Holy brothers are people set apart by Jesus Christ for God. That's who the saints are. We are not only brothers in Christ but we are also saints in Christ. In Christ we are set apart for God. Sainthood is the status of all believers. Even the Corinthians were called saints by Paul in First Corinthians 1:2 (KJV), and they were anything but saintly in much of their behavior. They were to live saintly lives, lives that were to be the expression of who they were and what Christ had made them.

Sometimes we have the idea, falsely, that saints are made saints by the church when they are canonized—which always happens after they die. I want to say to all of you people who read this today and who have believed in Jesus—you've already been "canonized." You have become saints because of your faith in Jesus Christ. You are a saint—now you are to live like a saint. We are to practice what we profess. We are to express who we are. Our position as saints must lead to our practice of saintliness. We have been separated out of this world positionally. We have been set apart to be the saints of God.

The fact is we are to live lives that reflect the holy character of Jesus Christ. When He comes to live in my heart He is going to live like He's always lived. He's going to be the Person He's always been and reflect and express the character that has always been there. And that character is a holy character. Faith in Christ makes us holy people.

Faith in Christ Gives Us Grace and Peace (1:2)

Faith in Christ gives us grace and peace: "Grace and peace to you from God our Father" (1:2). It is interesting to observe that we have grace in the second verse of this epistle and we have grace at the last verse of this epistle, so the whole epistle is framed by grace. And that is a wonderful word. It is pregnant with meaning for the believer and has many profound truths connected with it.

What does *grace* mean? It means God's free favor apart from all human merit. All of God's people have been graced. You're a graced person. You've come into favor with God through Christ.

Let me give you four simple things about grace as it relates to those who've placed their faith in Christ.

1. First of all, we're *saved by grace.* Ephesians 2:8 says, "For it is by grace you have been saved, through faith."

2. We're *gifted by grace.* "To each one of us grace has been given as Christ apportioned it" (Ephesians 4:7). You've been graced with a gift. Every single believer who reads this has been gifted by God almighty. In His grace He's given you a gift that is to function within His Church, a gift through which He will bless other people. I think it is very important for us to understand this and to say, "My life has meaning because Jesus Christ has graced me with a gift, and that gift has enormous value." It is to bless people, it is to be the instrument by which the will of the Lord is done. It is how I will reach out and touch other lives in meaningful and positive ways.

3. And then we are *enabled by grace.* Do we need enablement? Yes, we do. And God is rich in grace (1:7). The Bible says that Jesus is the man full of grace (John 1:14). You will find all the grace of God in Jesus. He is grace personified, and He gives us enabling grace in our desperate crises. When Paul felt weak, when he felt physically exhausted, when he felt that he could not go on, the Lord met him and said, "My grace is sufficient for you, for my power is made perfect in weakness" (2 Corinthians 12:9). My grace *is*—present tense, right here, right now, at this point, where you are, Paul—sufficient for you. Anyone who feels he's just sort of existing, who feels weak, incapable, somehow not up to his assignment—anyone that feels this way, this grace of Jesus Christ is for you. Take these words in your heart. God's grace is sufficient for you.

4. We are *sanctified by grace.* We read about the early Church in Acts 4:33: "Much grace was upon them all." This means that the Church was clothed with the beautiful garment of grace. To have the grace of God upon a church means many things, but one thing it means is this: we are gracious people. Is there anything worse than a sour Christian? Is there anything worse than a Christian who goes around criticizing, running people down and acting ugly? It is totally contrary to what God

intends for His children. Are we a gracious church? Do we embrace people with grace? Some churches have a period in the service where every person is embraced by another person and they say, "Grace and peace to you." Paul used these words as a prayer at the beginning, a little benediction at the outset. He wasn't going into any deep theological instruction here, but the profound quality of those two words is still there: "Grace and peace."

Peace. The world is going to pieces. Isn't it interesting that, after the peace accord has been agreed upon between the Israelis and the others, they then have to have bodyguards for each of the leaders because people are threatening to assassinate them for passing a peace agreement? Does that make sense? It just tells me we are not going to find peace in this world. There is no peaceful environment in which we can settle down. Everywhere we go there is conflict and war and violence. "Peace be with you!" said Jesus (John 20:19). The Lord Jesus gives us peace, but not as the world gives. He gives His own peculiar kind of peace.

The believer has *peace with God.* We can look into the face of God and know that He is smiling on us. Reconciliation has been made through the blood of the cross. We have been reconciled to God. There is peace with God (Romans 8:6). Then we have the *God of peace* (Philippians 4:9). He is not up there somewhere; He is living here within me. Then we have the *peace of God* (4:6-7). So we believers have in Christ peace with God, the God of peace and peace of God.

Faith in Christ Creates in Us a Love for His People (Colossians 1:4)

Faith in Christ also creates in us a love for His people. "We have heard of your faith in Christ Jesus and of the love you have for all the saints" (1:4). Faith in Christ and love for the saints go together.

The first is vertical and the second is horizontal. The first establishes relationship and the second expresses fellowship. The first brings us to the source of love—Jesus—and the second makes us channels of His love. The first is Christ-focused. We are placing our faith in Him. The second is church-focused. We are loving those whom He loves.

When we place our faith in Him we have a marvelous transformation of character. The Lord Jesus comes to live in our hearts and we begin to love what He loves because He expresses His character through us. Is Jesus loving His people today? How does He love His people today? For the most part He loves His people through His people.

Love is not primarily emotional nor erotic. Love is primarily the *agape* kind and is very practical. Does Ephesians 5:2 say, "Christ loved the Church and wrote love sonnets"? "Christ loved the Church and wrote a book about love and sent it to the Church"? "Christ loved the Church and talked about that love ceaselessly and endlessly"? No. "Christ loved us and gave himself up for us."

Years ago when I read that text, I said to myself, *Grout, if Jesus Christ loved the Church enough to die for it, you should love it enough to live for it. If He loved the Church enough to give Himself for it, you ought to love the Church enough to give yourself to it.* And long ago I was settled in my own conviction about where I would spend my ministry. I had other opportunities to serve the Lord, and I think I could have done it, but I chose the Church. I'll live and die in the Church. I am giving my life to the Church. I am giving my life to the Church because Jesus gave His life to the Church, set the example for me and, in a measure, has given me a love for His Church.

The Church is the community of love. This is where real love is known and expressed and experienced. It's not out there in the cold world. *This* is the community of love. We don't love as much as we should. We don't love as well as we should. There are many ways in which we need to increase in love, but we have the capacity, the potential, of loving people and expressing the very love of Christ to those people. Paul was writing to people who loved all the saints. It is significant that he said "all the saints." Sometimes we are a little selective in the saints we love. There are some saints who are not our type, but we are to love them. The Lord will help us to do that.

Faith in Christ Endows Us with a Heavenly Hope (Colossians 1:5)

" . . . the faith and love that spring from the hope that is stored up for you in heaven . . ." (1:5). All believers in Jesus are people of hope. Hope is the certain, joyous expectancy of the return of the Lord and all the eternal attendant blessings. Paul spoke about this as the "blessed hope" in Titus 2:13: ". . . while we wait for the blessed hope—the glorious appearing of our great God and Savior, Jesus Christ."

"While we wait for . . . " We are futurists if we are believers. What are we waiting for in the future? Are we looking for men to be able to work out all of their problems and get together and love one another and establish a lasting and a wonderful just order of government? Are we thinking that man is his own solution to his problems, that man will save himself? Are we looking for man to do better in the future? Are we looking for some age of peace ushered in through the instrumentality of bright minds and ardent souls? Are we expecting that the economies of the world will get better, that famine will be wiped off the face of the earth, that everyone sometime, somewhere, will have enough to eat and a place to sleep, and he will be loved and appreciated by the people around him?

Are we thinking that that is what is in the future for this world? Not in a thousand years. It will never come through man. It will never come through people no matter how rich or smart or good they are. Our hope is not in our ability to change anything permanently or eternally. Our hope is in the coming of Jesus Christ our Lord. It is the only hope this world has. And when He comes, the Prince of Peace will establish His throne and reign as King, and all the world will be in a state of peace. He will put down evil. He will judge evildoers. He will usher in a new age, an eternal age, where there will be a new heaven and a new earth wherein dwells righteousness.

I have given you a whole course in eschatology in three paragraphs, and I am only dealing with one little word: hope. It's our hope—Jesus is coming. It will be better ultimately, finally and eternally. In fact, it will be as good as God can make it.

This should not put us into neutral. We're salt and light, and we preach the gospel, come against evil, help people and build the Church. We put muscle and perspiration into this effort. We will show by our good works that we believe in what the Bible teaches. We will be good witnesses while we are looking for the blessed hope and glorious appearing of our great God and Savior Jesus Christ. We won't ever lose this hope because it's laid up and secured for us in heaven. We will always be people of hope. There are days when we don't hope as well as we might, but there is always that underlying, undergirding, foundational truth—I have a future. I have a wonderful future and I want to bring as many people into that future with me as I can. Hallelujah, we are people of hope.

Faith in Christ Joins Us with His Faithful Servants (Colossians 1:7)

Faith in Christ joins us with His faithful servants. How did the Colossians hear about the grace of God? How did they hear the truth? Colossians 1:5-7 gives the answer. Epaphras was the evangelist who brought the gospel to Colosse. He was the church builder who began the Colossian assembly. He was the pastor of this flock. He gave his life to these people. He was a marvelous servant of God and now he was a prisoner in Rome with Paul. But when you look at the last chapter you will discover that Epaphras kept right on in his pastoral responsibilities even though he was separated from his flock. "He is always wrestling in prayer for you, that you may stand firm in all the will of God, mature and fully assured" (4:12). That's a pastor's heart for his people. He wanted them to stand firm, to be fully assured, to understand and realize all that Christ had given to them. Epaphras was a man with a great zeal, a man of prayer, a great preacher, a great teacher, the servant of God and the servant to the church in Colosse.

They were a blessed people because of one man who gave himself unselfishly to them. Do you know that all of us are in God's family because of ministers? Are you glad for ministers? I am not speaking just about people who hold a theological degree and have the title Reverend. These people that ministered to the church in Colosse were an interesting group of people: Paul, Timothy, Epaphras, Aristarchus, Justus, Onesimus, Philemon and Tychicus. All kinds of people ministered to this church.

What brought this church into contact with all of these great ministers of Christ, these servants of God? It was their faith in Christ. When they came to the Lord they discovered that there were people out there who loved them, who cared for them, who were ministering to them, who were committed to their spiritual development. I'm in the ministry today because of ministers. I'm a pastor because of Wade K. Ramsey, a great teacher of theology. I'm here because of friends who prayed me through college. I'm here because of my parents. I am here today because of pastors. I am here today because I've read books. Every time I pull a book off my shelf a servant of Christ speaks to me from the page. He labored to put the words down. He prayed over that book and it is blessing me today, sometimes hundreds of years after it was written. We are all in the Church because of ministers. We are all believers because people loved us, cared for us, gave us the word of God, prayed us through when we were giving up on ourselves. I just want to say Hallelujah to God for all the ministers of Christ. We all ought to write at least a dozen thank-you notes this week or make a dozen phone calls to people who have loved us and ministered to our needs.

Faith in Christ Enables Us to Live in the Spirit (1:8)

Faith in Christ enables us to live in the Spirit. Notice the last expression in Colossians 1:8: "who also told us of your love in the Spirit." Paul said in Romans 8:9, "You are not in the flesh but in the spirit" (NKJV). He said in Galatians 5:25, "If we live in the Spirit, let us also walk in the Spirit" (NKJV). In Philippians 3:3 he said, "We . . . worship God in the Spirit" (NKJV). In Ephesians 6:18 he says we are to "pray in the Spirit." And in Revelation 1:10, John, on that rocky little island of Patmos being held as a prisoner for Christ, said, "On the Lord's Day I was in the Spirit." And because he was in the Spirit on the Lord's Day, God gave him a revelation of the Lord Jesus Christ that was never given to anyone before him and there hasn't been anything equal to it since. We should all be in the Spirit on the Lord's Day.

What does it mean to be in the Spirit? It means to be under the control of the Spirit, recognizing Him in your life. It means to understand that all your resources are in the Holy Spirit, that He will give you strength to love, to be true, to be pure and to be holy. We are to live in the Spirit and walk in the Spirit. The Spirit is the dynamic of the Christian Church. These Colossians were loving in the Spirit; He was pouring out, in their hearts, the love of Christ.

Questions for Reflection or Discussion

1. Faith in Christ brings us into a spiritual brotherhood (Colossians 1:2). This brotherhood is found in a Person—"in Christ"—but it functions at a place—"at Colosse." What is your Colosse? Can people see that you belong to a spiritual brotherhood?

2. Faith in Christ makes us holy people. The believers at Colosse were addressed as "holy and faithful brothers." What does it mean to live a holy life?

3. Faith in Christ gives us grace and peace. What are four ways that a believer experiences God's grace? What are the three dimensions of peace that a believer has?

4. Faith in Christ creates in us a love for His people.

    Faith in Christ is _____.
    Love for all the saints is _____.
    Faith establishes _____.
    Love expresses _____.
    Faith brings us to the _____.
    Love for the saints makes us the _____ of love.
    Faith is _____-focused.
    Love is _____-focused.

5. Faith in Christ endows us with a heavenly hope. Define hope. Is our hope secure? Explain.

6. Faith in Christ joins us with His faithful servants. Name some of the servants Paul listed in this epistle. Give the ministry of one.

7. Faith in Christ enables us to live in the Spirit. What are some of the things we as believers are to do in the Spirit?

Endnote

1. William Barclay, *The Letters to the Philippians, Colossians, and Thessalonians,* Daily Bible Studies (Toronto, ON: Welch Co., 1956), pp. 104-105.

2

Christic
The Answer to Our Prayers

Colossians 1:9-14

For this reason, since the day we heard about you, we have not stopped praying for you and asking God to fill you with the knowledge of his will through all spiritual wisdom and understanding. And we pray this in order that you may live a life worthy of the Lord and may please him in every way: bearing fruit in every good work, growing in the knowledge of God, being strengthened with all power according to his glorious might so that you may have great endurance and patience, and joyfully giving thanks to the Father, who has qualified you to share in the inheritance of the saints in the kingdom of light. For he has rescued us from the dominion of darkness and brought us into the kingdom of the Son he loves, in whom we have redemption, the forgiveness of sins.

The theme of Colossians is the supremacy and the sufficiency of the Lord Jesus Christ. "Christ is all, and is in all" (3:11). Jesus is all we need. That is the basis for Paul's prayer. He is praying to this all-sufficient Christ and Christ is indeed the answer to our prayers. Have you thought of it that way? Have you thought that Jesus Christ is the answer to your prayer? He can meet the total need of your life. Whether in the physical realm, the financial realm, the emotional realm or the spiritual realm, the Lord Jesus Christ is more than enough for you and He will be more than enough for you for time and forever.

When I look at Paul's prayer and consider my own prayer life, I am convicted. There is little comparison; it's mostly contrast. I find my prayers are focused on material things, focused on things that ultimately and finally won't matter in heaven. We pray so low. We are so in touch with the things of this world that often we overlook what we really should be praying for as we pray for one another. I should ask after I have prayed, "Will that prayer matter in heaven? If God should answer my prayer today, will it matter in eternity or is it just something that will pass away with the passing of time?"

The prayer Paul prayed is immortal. We have it on the page before us today. This prayer will live forever. This prayer has blessed, encouraged, helped, strengthened and sanctified millions of people for nearly 2,000 years of time. This is really a quality prayer that becomes to you and me an excellent pattern to follow. Please observe:

1. why Paul prayed
2. how Paul prayed
3. where Paul prayed
4. what Paul prayed.

Why Paul Prayed (1:9)

Paul prayed because he had received some important information from Epaphras. You will remember that Epaphras was a person who had come to know Christ as his Savior (we believe it was in Ephesus) and then went to Colosse. There he preached the gospel, people believed and a church was formed. Later he went from Colosse to Rome where Paul was in prison and he was imprisoned as well. When Paul wrote this letter, Epaphras was in prison with him in Rome. Paul learned from Epaphras everything he knew about the church in Colosse. One thing he knew was that these people had placed their faith in Jesus Christ. They were true believers. They had joined the family of God.

When Paul became aware of the Christians in Colosse he immediately began to pray for them. The information inspired his intercession. We need information to be effective in our praying. We do not pray well in a vacuum! Paul had never seen the Colossians, but they were really his spiritual grandchildren. Epaphras was his spiritual son, and he had led the Colossians to Christ; they became a third generation of Christians. He was praying for them because he learned of the good progress they were making in their Christian living. He celebrated that and he thanked God for it, but he prayed for them also because he had learned from Epaphras that a certain error was beginning to creep into their church.

We will see later in our study precisely what it was, but let me just say briefly that the error was saying something like this: Jesus alone is not enough. You need Jesus *and* asceticism. You need to be hard on yourself, go without food and sleep on a cold floor. That's the only way to serve Jesus. You've got to have some kind of self-inflicted pain if you're going to be a truly spiritual Christian. Or you need Jesus *and* mysticism. You must get involved in dreams and visions and the worship of angels. Or you need Jesus *and* legalism. You must add to your life rituals and the strict observances of dietary laws and certain feast days if you are to have the full blessing of God.

What is Paul's front line of defense against heresy? Prayer. He prayed first before he put pen to paper. Before he said one word to the Colossians he said many words about them and for them to the Father in heaven. Prayer is always first. I need to know that as a pastor. You need to know that too whether you're a pastor, teacher, parent or a person who is trying to help other people in their Christian living. We need to bring these people to the Lord in prayer. That is why Paul prays.

You will notice that his prayer was totally Christ-focused. He understood that Jesus and Jesus alone could meet the needs of the Christians in Colosse. This is a Christ-focused prayer. Everything he was asking God for on behalf of the Colossians will come to them in and through the person and the work of Jesus Christ.

Do you believe that it is a simplification to say that Jesus is all we need? It is a simple statement, but it is profound when you begin to understand what the Bible teaches about this infinitely and illimitably glorious Person. He is all you need.

How Paul Prayed (1:9)

Paul prayed without ceasing: "Since the day we heard about you, we have not stopped praying for you" (1:9). This doesn't mean, of course, that Paul was verbalizing a petition twenty-four hours a day. That would have been humanly impossible. It means that he prayed for these people and kept on praying for these people. He didn't pray once or twice and then stop. He kept at it.

He prayed with others. Paul was always in touch with other people. Paul always had people at his side he was discipling. He was always receiving from them too, being prayed for and being encouraged. He was always fellowshiping. When he prayed for the church at Colosse he wasn't sending up a prayer from his heart only; he was joining with another in this prayer. "Since the day we heard about you, *we* have not stopped praying for you" (1:9, emphasis added). Paul's prayer partner was

Epaphras. "Epaphras, who is one of you and a servant of Christ Jesus, sends greetings. He is *always wrestling in prayer for you*" (4:12, emphasis added). Keep in mind that Epaphras is in prison also. He too is separated from his flock. Oh, but he can be with them! He can be with them at the throne of grace. He can take that whole congregation and labor fervently in prayer on their behalf, even when he is absent from the church.

I think I pray more for my congregation when I am not there at the church than when I am. Somehow when you are away from people and you can't have a kind of hands-on ministry, you feel a responsibility and you say, "Lord, I'm not there, but You are. I can't help them, but You can. I can't be directly involved with them, but You can be directly involved with each one of my flock. Oh God, bless them, meet their needs, minister Yourself to them."

A wonderful kind of ministry comes by joining with others in prayer. Do you have a prayer partner? Do you have someone in this world that you feel intimate with to the extent that you can share confidential matters with them and they will not violate that confidence? Do you have a person who cares for you and you know he does? Do you have a person who is there for you when you need help, someone you can pray with about things you would never mention in a prayer meeting? This is one of the first things I ask people when they come to me for counsel. If they don't, I try to help them find one. Then that prayer partner joins with them and they are in fellowship in prayer together. All of us need prayer partners.

The Bible says, "Two are better than one" (Ecclesiastes 4:9). Isn't it interesting that in the Bible you have God doing things through pairs? Moses and Joshua. David and Jonathan. Elijah and Elisha. Paul and Timothy or Epaphras. Two are better than one. "If two of you on earth agree about anything you ask for, it will be done for you," Jesus said (Matthew 18:19). I urge you to get a prayer partner. It may be someone outside your church. It may be a colleague. It may be a friend. Who knows who it may be, but there is someone in this world that is matched up with you if you will only ask God to reveal who that person is. How did Paul pray? He prayed with a prayer partner.

He prayed before he did anything else. We cannot do anything before we pray. We can do many things after we pray but we must pray first. Paul brought these people before Christ and *then* he wrote them a letter. Heaven is always open. You'll never have a closed door into the throne room of the universe. The Lord sits there on a throne of grace to give you mercy and grace in time of need. Hallelujah forever! There is always a prayer opportunity. There is always the privilege of going to God in prayer, and what a great privilege it is.

Where Paul Prayed (Colossians 1:9)

Where did Paul pray? He prayed from a prison cell. That's a pretty bad environment. It's a pretty controlled environment. It's not a pleasant place to be. There was no privacy. He was chained to a Roman soldier and the soldier was there across the room from him. How would you like to do your devotions every day in the presence of a pagan Roman soldier? How would you like to talk to God with a man at the other end of the chain who didn't know God?

Some of us have difficulty with privacy. Some of us think we have to have a very comfortable little place, a kind of little sanctuary, where we can do our praying. There is value in having a pleasant place for prayer but it's not necessary. Some of the greatest praying you and I will ever do will be in the most unpleasant circumstances in life. Suppose Paul hadn't been locked up. We wouldn't have this letter and we wouldn't have his prayer and we wouldn't have this blessing. You see, when God put Paul in prison He opened to Paul a ministry that he never would have had otherwise.

He prayed hundreds of miles away from the Colossians. Distance is no hindrance when we pray for people. God is everywhere present at the same moment. I can pray here and God answers in Timbuktu. Prayer brings us into these enormous dimensions of God. I am limited to one place at one time, but God isn't. When I pray I bring His omnipotence and His omnipresence to bear upon the people for whom I pray.

When I touch God in prayer, that is when the Almighty expresses Himself in all of His attributes. That is when He works in ways that He doesn't work otherwise. Limitations create our greatest opportunity for prayer. If you feel limited—and all of us do in certain circumstances, certain situations—that is an opportunity for prayer. *I may not be able to talk directly to people about the Lord but I can always talk directly to the Lord about people.* Both of these are essential. When I talk to the Lord about people that's a priestly ministry. When I talk to people about the Lord that's a prophetic ministry. That is preaching Christ. These are always linked together in the Bible. C. Bridges said, "There can be little doubt but we shall find that our most successful hours of employment for our people were not those when we were speaking to them for God but when we were speaking to God for them."[1]

What Paul Prayed (1:9)

Paul's prayer was in three parts: the will of God; the walk with God; the worship of God. Paul incorporated all of these great thoughts into this prayer.

The will of God (1:9)

Paul prayed that God would "fill [them] with the knowledge of his will through all spiritual wisdom and understanding" (1:9). The implication of this petition is that knowing and doing the will of God do not come naturally. What would be the point of Paul praying that this would happen if it would happen anyway?

No, the natural thing is to do our will. My natural thing is to do my will to get what I want. I can even be selfish in my praying. I can be self-willed in my preaching. I can be self-willed in my pastoral duties. I can be self-willed in my family life. I can be controlled by self. That is the natural thing. The supernatural thing is when I begin to pray, "Your will be done on earth as it is in heaven" (Matthew 6:10).

In First Corinthians 2:13-14 we read,

> This is what we speak, not in words taught us by human wisdom but in words taught by the Spirit, expressing spiritual truths in spiritual words. The man without the Spirit does not accept the things that come from the Spirit of God, for they are foolishness to him, and he cannot understand them, because they are spiritually discerned.

The wisdom of God is a total mystery to the world. The wisdom of God is wisdom that He shares only with His children. We can have the mind of Christ. We can think thoughts after God. We can have His perspective. That is sacred philosophy. That is the wisdom of God, and Paul is praying that these believers in Colosse will have this wisdom which will enable them to know and do the will of God.

Prayer is never to change God's will or to persuade Him to do our will. Sometimes we think that way when we pray. We want to persuade God that there is something we need that He doesn't know about or something perhaps He is reluctant to give. So we get into this kind of arguing which is absolutely futile. Forget it—it's not going to work. That isn't praying. We never pray, "Thy will be changed." No, we pray, "Thy will be done." Who taught us to pray that? The Lord Jesus. Did He practice what He taught? Yes, in the garden, when He drank that bitter cup, when He took your guilt and mine upon Himself, He said, "Father, . . . not my will, but thine, be done" (Luke 22:42, KJV).

The whole scheme of salvation hinged on that prayer. Jesus did not come to do His will. He came to do the will of the Father who sent Him. The Bible says He delighted to do His will. Aren't you glad? Because Jesus did the will of the Father you and I have been redeemed. We are the children of God because one Man did the will of God. And every blessing that has come to the Church and through the Church all through its generations has come through people who were yielded to the will of God.

We are not here talking about just getting direction for our life. Finding the will of God is getting God's viewpoint. It is discovering what God thinks, reading what He has said and embracing the truth. It is coming to understand that God is doing something in the world, He has revealed it in His Word and He is here in the Person of the Holy Spirit to accomplish it. That is the will of God. It is irrelevant where it is done. The important thing is not geography but that I embrace the will of God for me. That's what Paul was praying about: we need wisdom to know His will, discover His mind, learn His perspective.

We need His wisdom and we also need understanding. Understanding is knowing how to carry out His will once it is discovered. It is really applied wisdom. It is coming to know what is in God's mind, what's in God's heart, what's important to Him, embracing that, whatever it is, and then saying, "Lord, give me understanding as to how this will work itself out in my day-to-day living." Wisdom and understanding are both essential in knowing the will of God.

The walk with God (Colossians 1:10)

Then we have not only the will of God, but also the walk with God. "That you may live a life worthy of the Lord" (1:10). The

NKJV says, "That you may walk worthy of the Lord." Walk, in Paul's use of the word, relates to behavior. It relates to the way I live, the way I conduct myself. He is praying that these Colossians will behave day by day, in the marketplace, in the home, on the streets—wherever they go—in a way that is pleasing to the Lord.

The Lord is worthy of our best. We are to reflect in the way we live that He is worthy. We have named Him Lord of our lives—now we want to show that we really do value Him, that He has great worth to us, by the way we conduct ourselves. We sing "He is worthy" all the time. He is worthy of all that I can give Him. He is worthy of all that I can do for Him. He is worthy of all of my praise. He is worthy of all of my service. He is worthy of my life, lock, stock and barrel. Only Jesus is worthy. We don't give ourselves to service, organizations or people in the same way that we give ourselves to Christ. He is worthy of the best we can give.

Our walk is to be fully pleasing to Him: "You . . . may please him in every way" (1:10). I have had men come to me often and say, "Pastor, in all of my life I never did a thing that pleased my dad. I was always a failure in his eyes. He never affirmed me. He never loved me. He has never said he was pleased with me." Some of you have never felt that your fathers were pleased. For that matter, you have questioned whether your life has pleased anyone. I want you to get out of that bondage by putting your finger on Colossians 1:10. I want you to know that you can please the Father. You can look up into His face every day of your life and say, "Father, I know You're pleased. I know You smile with favor upon me." What an enormous blessing that is. We have the privilege of pleasing God—we can do it by His grace. We can live lives that are pleasant to Him.

Our walk is to be characterized by fruitful works (1:10). All of us want our lives to produce something that matters. But how do we do it? By simply abiding in the Vine, the Lord Jesus

Christ (John 15). All of us believers are branches which draw from Him, from His life, from His fruit-producing ability. We draw from Him our vitality and everything we need as branches. Then we bear fruit. We don't produce it—the vine produces it. We just bear it. That is not just a play on words. That is a theological distinction of profound consequences. We have a connection to Him.

Are we fruitful? Are we bearing fruit? Is the Lord producing something through us that will please the Father? The husband-man, the vine keeper, the Father, might have fruit from His vineyard.

Our walk is to be energized by His might and glorious power. Notice it says, "strengthened with all power according to his glorious might" (Colossians 1:11). The Lord hasn't just said, "Now go to it. Do your best and I'll be watching and hoping that things work out." No, we are energized, we are strengthened by the very presence and power of almighty God in order to walk a life that is pleasing to Him. Paul wrote another letter from the prison in Rome and in that letter to the church at Philippi He said, "I can do all things through Christ who strengthens me" (Philippians 4:13, NKJV). Isn't that a great text? What lies in the will of God for you? What is it that God has called you to do? What role are you to fill? What ministry are you to have? Whatever it is, you can do it through the strength that Jesus Christ gives. You can finish your course with joy. You can do your assignment. You can do what He has appointed you to do.

Did you notice what all this strength, power and might are all about? For "great endurance and patience" (Colossians 1:11). God's power is at your disposal to make you patient. You say, "Big deal." You need it, though, don't you? I do. If there's anything I need, it's patience in circumstances over which I have no control. Sometimes I get the feeling that I am victimized. Do you ever feel that way? You need patience in those circumstances. You need to be longsuffering with people—people you don't like or don't like you, people who rub you the wrong way, people who are socially maladjusted, people who are sometimes a real pest. God's power will make us endure our circumstances and be patient with people. We won't grit our teeth and say, "I am patient." It will be done joyfully.

The worship of God (1:12)

Now the last thought: the worship of God. After the petition, after asking, Paul said, "giving thanks" (1:12). Prayer is more than asking. Prayer is thanking. We not only come to the throne of grace to receive; we also come to the throne of grace to give. This is where the prayer climaxes—not in petition but in worship, giving thanks to the Father. How important that is. Paul gave thanks because of four wonderful blessings.

1. God has qualified us to be partakers of a rich inheritance. Paul said that we are heirs of God and joint heirs with Jesus Christ—what a wonderful thing! As children we become heirs in the family, joint heirs with our elder brother Jesus. Heirs of God.

2. He has rescued us from the power or dominion of darkness. You are a delivered person today if you have believed in Jesus, no longer under the authority of this dark world or of Satan. Just as God took His people from the power of Pharaoh in Egypt, set them free and brought them into the Promised Land, so He has taken you and me out from under the authority of a despot. We don't belong to this world anymore. We are not a part of its system. We have been delivered out of it. H.M. Carson says:

> The realm in which we were slaves is described as *darkness.* This implies not only absence of light, but opposition to the light. It is not only a condition of being without God, but of being against God. Hence we

have been delivered from a rebel kingdom, and brought under the sovereignty of our rightful King. Just as a conqueror in the ancient world often transplanted an entire people to a new land, so our heavenly Conqueror has uprooted the people of God from alien soil and brought them to the liberty of their true homeland.[2]

3. He has brought us or translated us into the kingdom of the Son He loves. We are in a kingdom with a loving King. The Son of God's love is our sovereign. We are children in the kingdom of God.

4. He has redeemed us through His blood and given us the forgiveness of sins. He has bought us with a price. He has purchased us to be His people.

All of these four wonderful things were in Paul's mind when he gave thanks.

Questions for Reflection or Discussion

1. Why can we be confident that Christ is the answer to our prayers?
2. What was necessary before Paul could pray intelligently for the Colossian Christians?
3. Explain Paul's first line of defense against heresy.
4. Who was Paul's prayer partner? What was his partner's role in the church at Colosse?
5. Discuss how Paul's limited circumstances enhanced his prayer life. Do you pray best when things are pleasant or unpleasant? Why?
6. Discuss the three areas where Paul is making petition to the Lord.
7. How does Paul's prayer climax?

8. After studying this inspired prayer, list some ways your prayer life can improve.

Endnotes

1. C. Bridges, quoted in H.C.G. Moule, *Colossians Studies* (New York: D.D. Hodder and Stoughton, 1898), p. 46.
2. H.M. Carson, *Colossians and Philemon,* Tyndale New Testament Commentaries (Leicester, England: InterVarsity, 1960), p. 40.

3

Christ: Created and Redeemed by Him

Colossians 1:15-23a

He is the image of the invisible God, the firstborn over all creation. For by him all things were created: things in heaven and on earth, visible and invisible, whether thrones or powers or rulers or authorities; all things were created by him and for him. He is before all things, and in him all things hold together. And he is the head of the body, the church; he is the beginning and the firstborn from among the dead, so that in everything he might have the supremacy. For God was pleased to have all his fullness dwell in him, and through him to reconcile to himself all things, whether things on earth or things in heaven, by making peace through his blood, shed on the cross.

Once you were alienated from God and were enemies in your minds because of your evil behavior. But now he has reconciled you by Christ's physical body through death to present you holy in his sight, without blemish and free from accusation—if you continue in your faith, established and firm, not moved from the hope held out in the gospel.

This is one of those texts that are too big for us preachers. These are truths that simply cannot in any perfect way be verbalized. They are truths around which we cannot stretch our little minds. They are truths we believe but truths we will continue to learn from and about forever. Jesus is an inexhaustible subject. No one ever fully understands or fully embraces or fully knows this infinite Person. And that is brought to our attention in a very dramatic way in the passage before us.

The apostle Paul did not clearly define for us the heresy that was creeping into the church at Colosse. We do know that false teachers were making inroads and teaching things contrary to the gospel. Paul said some things in the epistle that cause us to believe that he was addressing the error of gnosticism. The word "gnostic" comes from the Greek word for knowledge. The gnostics were people who believed they had knowledge superior to that of ordinary Christians. They believed that there were only a few initiates, only a few who got on the inside and really understood this full knowledge of truth.

They had an interesting dichotomy. They believed that the universe is divided between the material and the spiritual. They did not believe that God created the universe, but rather an evil force did, so that all material things were reflective of this evil force that had brought them into existence. All material things were evil because they had a bad origin. On the other hand, they believed that all spiritual things, all things that were invisible, all things in the spirit realm, were good.

Now of course they had a problem with Jesus because Jesus had a physical body. They had to explain it away and so they simply said that He was a phantom that gave a physical appearance. In other words, He was an apparition. You saw what you thought was a body but there really wasn't a body there. Some of them even said that when He walked on the seashore, He didn't leave footprints. This was the dichotomy of the gnostics.

Not only did they believe these things, but they also believed that Jesus Christ was not sufficient to save people by Himself. They had a strange doctrine of angels. They believed that there were a large number of angels who served with Jesus as intermediaries. Jesus alone could not save people; He needed the assistance of all of these angels to help Him in the work of redemption.

I am sure you're not all that impressed with some of these basic things they believed, so I won't go into their other strange doctrines. But this is enough to give us some understanding as to why Paul was laying such heavy emphasis on certain truths concerning Christ in this wonderful letter.

Apart from the gnostics, apart from the error, this is inspired Scripture, and the apostle Paul was given the ability to say things he has never said anywhere else, to say things that have scholars still probing to learn what he meant. He is saying things in this passage of Scripture that we would have a difficult time believing if they weren't in the Word of God. We are dealing here with some profound and infinite spiritual dimensions beyond our ability to understand fully. That doesn't mean we do not believe these truths—we do. We embrace them and say, "Lord Jesus, You are an unsearchable person. You are an infinite person. You are a person without human dimensions. You are a person so immense and so great and so glorious in all of Your attributes that we are just beginning to learn about You and we want to learn more and more about You. We want to continue this learning process throughout all the ages of eternity."

The Lord Jesus Christ is the person upon whom we focus just now. We are going to do two things: We are going to take the profound statements in our passage and observe what is said about who Christ is (His person) and then we are going to observe what they say about what He has done (His works). We are focused on who He is and we are focused on how He expresses Himself and what He has done in history.

First of all then, let's discover from Paul . . .

Who Christ Is . . . His Person

He is the image of the invisible God (1:15).

He Himself, He alone, is the image of the invisible God. When men try to make images of God they always degrade and dishonor Him. Only Christ is the perfect representation of almighty God. He is the only one who reflects and expresses in a perfect way who God is. One day Jesus, the Nazarene carpenter turned prophet, stood before Phillip, one of His disciples, and said, "Anyone who has seen me has seen the Father" (John 14:9). On the lips of any other person, these would be words of blasphemy of the rankest order. Jesus was saying, "Look on Me, and in My image you will see the image, the reflection, the expression, the manifestation of the invisible God. You will see in My love the love of God. You will see in My mercy the mercy of God. You will see in My character the character of God. You will see in My strength the strength of God. You will see in My purity the purity of God. Whatever you see in Me it is a reflection of God Almighty."

You will recall, back in the Garden, that Adam, the first man, turned away from the Lord, disobeyed His word, became a rebel and was cast out of the Garden. The Bible tells us that Adam was created in the image of God. That means that he reflected God's character, God's personality and something of the moral attributes of almighty God. He didn't reflect a physical being because God is Spirit, without arms and legs and a face.

But we know that Adam sinned and that image of God was marred, and Adam led the whole human race into sin. All of us are sons and daughters of Adam and we have the image of our fallen father. But the last Adam—the Lord Jesus—has come to restore the image. He has come, indeed, to be the image of the invisible God, and the ultimate purpose in redemption is to transform us mortal and fallen beings into His image or likeness. Note Romans 8:29: "For those God foreknew he also predestined to be conformed to the likeness of his Son, that he might be the firstborn among many brothers." The ultimate in God's redemption is that you and I will reflect the image of Jesus Christ forever. The image is restored in the last Adam. Isn't that a staggering thought? "We shall be like him, for we shall see him as he is" (1 John 3:2), John said. We shall be like Jesus Christ, in whom we have the perfect image of the invisible God. We shall look like Jesus—as much as the grace and power of God can make us look like Jesus—forever!

He is the firstborn over all creation (Colossians 1:15).

Firstborn means to have priority in time and supremacy in position. Jesus was there first. He was God's only begotten Son. He was not created; He was begotten. He was there first and He is over all that follows in creation.

He is before all things (1:17).

In time and space Jesus Christ is always first. He is always prior. He is always before all that follows. Christ had eternal existence before anything was created. "In the beginning was the Word, and the Word was with God, and the Word was God" (John 1:1). Jesus was in the beginning and all things were created by Him.

He is the one in whom all things consist (Colossians 1:17).

He is the one in whom all things consist, or hold together, or cohere. We have a cosmos of order and not of chaos because Jesus is holding all things together. Whether the atomic structure of matter or the movements of galaxies and stars 2 billion light years away, Jesus is holding the material universe together. He is holding nature together. It is a wonderful thing to know that the Lord Jesus has established the laws of nature. We have hydrogen and oxygen combined to make water. Separate them and you have two of the most explosive gases known to men. This whole universe would blow apart if Jesus were not holding it together.

Now if He can hold the universe together, He can hold your life together. He can hold your marriage together. He can hold your church together. He can hold your business together. He is the integrating personality. He is the one who brings all things, and people, together.

Deists have the theory that when God created the universe He set in place certain natural laws and then removed Himself from the universe. We are controlled by those laws, but God has nothing to do with you, has nothing to do with me. We are the victims of a closed system. Well, the deists don't know what they're talking about. The Lord Jesus *is* transcendent, above all things—all principalities, all powers, all thrones, all forces, all people. He is above all the forces of the universe. He is up there exalted on the throne above all. He is transcendent but He is also immanent. That means that He is not only up there but also down here. He is involved in all of the political and social movements of society, all of the wars and rumors of wars. Jesus Christ is present on planet earth and He is involved and He is holding things together.

Here is some "Groutology" for you: this is not in any theology book and you can take it with a grain of salt. I believe that men would self-destruct were it not for the fact that Jesus is holding all things together. Man will never destroy himself, and the reason is not because he is not bad enough to do it but because Jesus won't permit it to happen. Jesus is going to come back to an intact earth. He is going to take all the evil forces that are trying to destroy themselves and He is going to put them down. King Jesus is going to establish His throne—He is going to rule in this world. Then there will be a visible manifestation of the truth of our text. One day in history Jesus will be on the throne holding all things together. He is the integrating personality. He gives coherence to fragmentation. He gives coherence to a world that's breaking apart.

He is the head of the body—the Church (1:18).

He is not only the firstborn over all creation but He is the head of the new creation and of His body, the Church. Jesus creates two things—only two. He doesn't create business, He doesn't create educational institutions, He doesn't create religious organizations. Jesus creates the universe and He creates the Church. We are the new creation. The Bible says, "If anyone is in Christ, he is a new creation; the old has gone, the new has come!" (2 Corinthians 5:17). Isn't it marvelous to be a part of the new creation, the Church? After heaven and earth have passed away the new creation will be there, bright and beautiful, shining in all the glory of its creator, Jesus. He's our head, the head of the Church. He is supreme in both the physical and spiritual realms. He is the one source of our strength, of our wisdom, of our authority in the Church. The head of our Church is not in Toronto or Colorado Springs, sitting behind a mahogany desk with only human resources. The Lord Jesus Christ is the head of the Church.

Just as my head takes in nourishment for my body, so all of us must take our nourishment from Jesus Christ. Just as my head gives impulses so that my physical body will move and function harmoniously, so Jesus will give His spiritual body His impulses. Jesus will give us His wisdom. Jesus will give His direction to us as a church. This is absolutely vital for us to understand. The Board of Elders and the pastoral staff are not the heads of the church. They can't sustain it, they can't keep it, they can't prosper it, they can't bless it. They can only point

His people to Him who can. That is their ministry, their responsibility.

Jesus is the head. We should sing His praise. We should give
Him honor. We should say, "Jesus, You are the head of the
Church. Lead us and do with us as You please. We are Your
body. Live in us, function in us, teach us, heal us, bless us,
preach through us and do whatever You want to do. You are the
head and You alone have the prerogative of expressing Your
life and doing Your will."

He is the beginning, the firstborn from the dead (Colossians 1:18).

Not only are we a part of a Church, but we are part of a
family. Jesus is the firstborn. "Firstborn" indicates that He is
the beginning, and "beginning" denotes more than just first in a
series. It means also the source to which the series can be
traced. He is the beginning of all the children of God within the
household of faith. He's the one who leads the family of God.
He is the firstborn, the person who has priority in that relationship.

He is the One who in all things has preeminence or supremacy (1:18).

When I pastored in Minnesota, above the chancel in our
sanctuary were these words, "That in all things He might have
the preeminence." When I stepped onto the platform, often I
looked at those words and I said to myself, *Grout, this morning,
Jesus and Jesus alone is to have preeminence and supremacy in
this church. Not you, the pastor, not the musicians, not the congregation. Jesus Christ is to have preeminence.*

He's the only man in the universe who is worthy of being
first. The only one. First in heaven, first on earth, first in time,
first in eternity, first in all places, at all times, over all people.
He is not first among equals; He is first—period. He is a class

all by Himself. He is not one king among many kings, one savior among many saviors, one master among many masters. He is *the* Master. He is *the* Savior. He is *the* Lord and as such He has all preeminence. You and I will never be number one. I get amused at these athletes who leap around and hold up their forefinger and shout, "We're number one." I've got news for you: there aren't any number ones in this world. I don't care how wealthy you are, how smart you are, how high you go on the social ladder, how far you go in your company or whatever you achieve in this world—you will never be number one. There is only one who is always number one . . . that's Jesus. Hallelujah.

He is the One in whom all fullness dwells (1:19).

Here is where we touch truth so deep, with such great dimensions, that I can just tell you what it says and let the Holy Spirit help you understand what it means. In this one Person, Jesus, dwells *all*, all the fullness *(pleroma* in the Greek).

Fullness denotes the sum total of all the powers, attributes, glories and blessings of God Almighty. They are all to be found, in perfection, in the Person of Jesus Christ. All that God is He is in His Son. All that God knows He knows in His Son. All that God does He does in His Son. All that God feels He feels in His Son. It helps us greatly to know that the Person in whom we have placed our faith, the Person we are following, is a Person in whom all the fullness of God dwells. Is there anything too hard for Him? Is there any problem too complex? Is there any burden too heavy? Are there any needs too great?

Oh, beloved people who read this, I urge you to come to the full Person. So many of us are so empty, so bankrupt. He is full. He is full of all that God is. You have all God's fullness in one Person.

Little wonder that we want to exalt Him and preach Him and teach Him and praise Him and worship Him. Little wonder that we say to each of you, "Christ is Savior, Sanctifier, Healer and coming King—He's everything!" A.B. Simpson said it so well in his poem "Himself":

> Once it was the blessing, now it is the Lord;
> Once it was the feeling, now it is His Word;
> Once His gift I wanted, now the Giver own;
> Once I sought for healing, now Himself alone.[1]

What Christ Has Done . . . His Works

All things were created by Him and for Him (1:16).

"For by him all things were created: things in heaven and on earth, visible and invisible, whether thrones or powers or rulers or authorities; all things were created by him and for him" (1:16). He is the source of all things. He is the agent of all things. He is the goal of all things. There is great theology here.

He is the conditioning cause, the mediating cause, the final cause for all things. This places enormous value on *things.* Some may say, "You're talking about something I'm interested in when you're talking about *things.*" I'm not talking about *your* things, though. I'm talking about *His* things. You have things as a trustee, not a consumer. All that you have Jesus created. Whatever it is, it came from Him.

Do you know what would happen if we really believed this text? Most of us would turn away from this page and totally re-evaluate our finances and worldly possessions. We would totally reevaluate our houses, our cars, our boats, our investments or whatever else we have been accumulating. But in another place Paul said, "God . . . richly provides us with everything for our enjoyment" (1 Timothy 6:17). We are to enjoy the things He has given us! We are to celebrate. We are to praise Him. We are to enjoy the material blessings we have. But we are always to recognize that He gave them, He created them and He has prior claim on everything I own. In fact, should I use the word "own"? I am only a trustee of all *He* owns. Everything is sacred. The gnostics in Colosse said all *things* were bad because they were material. The gnostics were wrong. All things are sacred because Jesus Christ created them. And I must not touch anything in this world without the understanding that I am a trustee, a steward of God's creation.

That can be applied as broadly as you want. Conservationists certainly can relate to this text. It touches our farmlands, forests, waters—everything in this world. He created them. He is to receive them for His praise and glory. He created not only a visible universe but He created an invisible universe. Do you know that there are many things invisible to us that Jesus created? He created principalities and powers. All the angels are invisible. He created them. He created them in ranks of power. There are archangels and others serving under them. This entire hierarchy was created by Jesus.

I believe He created the governing and political systems of men. Jesus is the Governor above all governors, the King above all kings, the Ruler above all rulers. He created them for Himself. And someday soon when He returns, He will take to Himself His great power and rule over all the kingdoms of this world (Revelation 11:15). He rules and overrules indirectly and through various agents now. But in that glorious future day, He will sit as King of kings and Lord of lords and reign supremely.

He reconciles (Colossians 1:20-22).

Reconciliation is also a part of what Jesus has done:

> and through him to reconcile to himself all things, whether things on earth or things in heaven, by making peace through his blood, shed on the cross.
>
> Once you were alienated from God and were enemies in your minds because of your evil behavior. But

> now he has reconciled you by Christ's physical body
> through death. . . . (1:20-22)

By him all things and all people are reconciled to God. Reconciliation is the removal of all estrangements or barriers. In all other religions men try to be reconciled to God by their own efforts, by ritual, by good works! Sometimes they even afflict their own bodies, trying to suffer for their sins. *They* try to reconcile themselves to God. Forget it! Only Jesus Christ can reconcile us to God, and He did it at the cross. The text says it's through the blood of the cross, through a physical body. He suffered for your sins and mine. And those of us who were enemies of God He has now reconciled.

He presents us to God holy, blameless and free from accusation (1:22).

Finally, by Him we will be presented to God, perfect—"holy in his sight, without blemish and free from accusation" (1:22). There is coming a day when we will be holy and blameless and irreproachable. Jesus, our advocate, is with the Father and He answers the accuser, the devil. He might accuse us, but in Christ there is no reproach. There is no accusation that will stand up against what Jesus Christ has done for you and me. He has saved us, He has redeemed us, He has justified us, He has reconciled us, He has done it all through His precious blood. He has suffered in our place. He took our judgment and set us free. In commenting on this passage, A.T. Robertson quotes Maclaren: "The end of all the majesty of creation and all the wonders of grace is that His solitary figure may stand clearly out as centre and Lord of the Universe, and His name be lifted high over all."[2]

I wish somehow I could make these truths come through this clay vehicle of mine with greater clarity, greater meaning and greater blessing. Nothing helps us understand our mortality and limitations more than when we come to these great themes. May the gracious Spirit help us grasp them, believe them and apply them.

Questions for Reflection or Discussion

1. Explain why the gnostics had a problem with Christ.
2. What does it mean when Paul said that Jesus is "the image of the invisible God"?
3. Does this have anything to do with our "image"?
4. How does this passage show that Jesus is the integrating personality of all things?
5. What are two ways that we benefit from the headship of Christ in the Church?
6. Where does God dwell in fullness? Does this have any practical significance in your life?
7. Name three great things Jesus has done for us.
8. How have these three impacted your life? What differences have they made?

Endnotes

1. A.B. Simpson, *Himself* (Camp Hill, PA: Christian Publications, 1991), p. 13.
2. Alexander Maclaren, quoted in A.T. Robertson, *Paul and the Intellectuals* (Nashville, TN: Broadman Press, 1956), p. 53.

4

Christ: Preaching (Proclaiming) Him

Colossians 1:23b-2:3

This the gospel that you heard and that has been proclaimed to every creature under heaven, and of which I, Paul, have become a servant.

Now I rejoice in what was suffered for you, and I fill up in my flesh what is still lacking in regard to Christ's afflictions, for the sake of his body, which is the church. I have become its servant by the commission God gave me to present to you the word of God in its fullness—the mystery that has been kept hidden for ages and generations, but is now disclosed to the saints. To them God has chosen to make known among the Gentiles the glorious riches of this mystery, which is Christ in you, the hope of glory.

We proclaim him, admonishing and teaching everyone with all wisdom, so that we may present everyone perfect in Christ. To this end I labor, struggling with all his energy, which so powerfully works in me.

I want you to know how much I am struggling for you and for those at Laodicea, and for all who have not met me personally. My purpose is that they may be encouraged in heart and united in love, so that they may have the full riches of complete understanding, in

order that they may know the mystery of God, namely, Christ, in
whom are hidden all the treasures of wisdom and knowledge.

In the passage before us, the apostle Paul digressed somewhat in his instruction to the church at Colosse and gave them something about his personal service of proclaiming or preaching Christ (1:23, 28).

He also reminded the church that they had had the gospel preached to them and that they must not move away from the hope that this gospel gives (1:23). Epaphras was probably the instrument that God used as the proclaimer or preacher to the people of Colosse.

Preachers are essential in the work of God. Sometimes secular minds are very critical of those of us who are called to preach. Preaching is often viewed as an outmoded method of communication. However, if we keep our biblical and historical perspective, we will see that preaching has always been one of God's primary ways to disseminate the truth. Paul said it so eloquently: "For since in the wisdom of God the world through its wisdom did not know him, God was pleased through the foolishness of what was preached to save those who believe" (1 Corinthians 1:21).

We can break in at any point in history and see how vital the preaching of God's Word has been. The prophets were preachers. The apostles were preachers. The early church fathers were preachers. The reformers were preachers. There have been great preachers in the modern era. And, of course, we must be constantly reminded that our blessed Lord Himself was a great preacher—indeed, the pattern preacher for all preachers. Consider with me six important factors as we think of what Paul said regarding his preaching ministry.

The Servanthood Factor (Colossians 1:23, 25)

Paul refers to himself as a servant twice in this passage. Other translations use the word "minister." Paul was saying that he was a servant of Jesus Christ, a servant to the Church—always a servant. The true preacher is not a spiritual boss, a benevolent dictator nor a lord over God's flock. He is not out to make a name for himself or get into a large church in order to gain a big salary. He is a servant, a servant who preaches and leads God's people and always takes the posture of a servant in his leadership. He never tells people what to do. He doesn't harangue. He doesn't boss people around. He doesn't "pull rank." He doesn't say, "You've got to do this because I happen to be the senior pastor." He serves from a posture of a servant.

Servanthood is so important. The Lord Jesus Christ, the Prince of all preachers, the Pastor of all pastors, has given to us an example without parallel. Jesus says, in Mark 10:45, "The Son of Man did not come to be served, but to serve, and to give his life as a ransom for many."

Many heartaches could be avoided in our churches today if all of us preachers were servants first of all. A true servant is never a threat to anyone. A true servant never abuses or calls attention to himself. He never demands honor or praise. His only desire is to serve the Lord by preaching the gospel of His saving grace.

The Suffering Factor (Colossians 1:24)

I know so little of suffering, but Paul knew much of it. In the first-generation Church there were many, many martyrs. We believe that all of the apostles, with the possible exception of one, died as a martyr to Jesus Christ. They not only ministered through their lips, they also ministered through their lives. They laid them down for Jesus just as Jesus had laid down His life for them.

I may have the privilege someday of suffering as a preacher of the gospel. So far I have had some criticism and there have been people who haven't appreciated my ministry, but for the most part there has been little severe opposition or suffering.

In contrast, Paul was writing this with a chain on his wrist— he was in a prison cell. There was an executioner's block about ten paces outside the cell door, and he knew that he was under the sentence of death for Jesus' sake. He certainly knew something about the preacher's suffering. He said in 1:24, "Now I rejoice in what was suffered for you, and *I fill up in my flesh what is still lacking in regard to Christ's afflictions,* for the sake of his body, which is the church" (emphasis added).

Jesus has suffered in two bodies. He suffered in His physical body on the cross to save us from our sins. That was a vicarious suffering. He will never suffer that way again. But He suffers now in His mystical body, the Church. When you hurt the body of Christ, you hurt Jesus Himself. Paul said, in essence, "I am filling up what is lacking in the afflictions of Christ." There is more suffering for Jesus to go through. He is suffering through me, He is suffering through His Body. This is a vital part of ministry. Christ suffered vicariously to provide salvation— now as His servants we must suffer experientially to preach salvation.

Jesus spoke of this in the beatitudes when He said this:

> Blessed are those who are persecuted because of
>   righteousness,
>   for theirs is the kingdom of heaven.
>
> Blessed are you when people insult you, persecute you and falsely say all kinds of evil against you because of me. Rejoice and be glad, because great is your reward in heaven, for in the same way they persecuted the prophets who were before you. (Matthew 5:10-12)

Jesus says that when we suffer for Him, it's a privilege; we must rejoice in that privilege. Paul was writing about rejoicing here in Colossians 1:24 when he said, "I rejoice in what was suffered for you."

This means that suffering for Christ is always a positive experience, just as His suffering for us was positive. It seemed negative. It seemed a terrible miscarriage of justice, which it was. It seemed the most horrible thing that could ever happen in the world—the Son of God dying with spittle on His face, nails in His hands and feet, dying there as a common criminal would die. It seemed bad on the surface, but everything positive, blessed, holy and good that you and I will ever know in this world or eternity comes to us from that bloody cross. If God Almighty can turn the sufferings of His Son into salvation for you, into blessing for you, into heaven for you, He can turn your sufferings into something very positive as well—so we rejoice in our sufferings.

The Stewardship Factor (1:25)

Paul said in 1:25: "I became a minister according to the stewardship from God which was given to me for you" (NKJV). Paul considered his preaching ministry a stewardship from God. He was the churches' servant through a special commission, a special assignment, a special call. No true preacher ever decides on his own to enter the ministry. He enters the ministry through a special call and through the unique grace and gifts of God.

When I was eighteen I shared with my father that I felt God was leading me into the ministry. My dad, who at the time was not a believer but had been raised in a Free Methodist parsonage, said, "Son, be sure you are called, because the ministry is not like any other profession. You don't decide to be a minister; it is decided for you. There is a decision that is higher than your decision. There is a call that is higher than your feelings. You must be called into ministry." Wasn't that great counsel from my father? Later he did embrace Jesus, and whenever I preached in the vicinity where he lived he was front and center, "amening" me all the way through. He was a great lover and affirmer and supporter of me. I bless his memory today.

We preachers must have an understanding that we are stewards of the grace of God. We are trustees of the gospel. We did not decide this; it was decided for us. Paul said it so eloquently in Ephesians 3:7: "I became a servant of this gospel by the gift of God's grace"! (Notice he didn't say, "I entered the ministry.") We must *become* a minister by the grace of God and then we minister.

To those ignorant, common, provincial fishermen, Jesus said, "Come, follow me, . . . and I will make you fishers of men" (Matthew 4:19). He didn't say, "Come after Me and I will teach strategy or methodology or how to fish." He said, "Follow Me and I will *make you* what you would never become on your own."

All of the men who followed Him are household words today—Peter, James, John, Andrew. We know them all. They became preachers; they didn't decide to enter the professional ministry. They became servants of Jesus Christ and they reflected His character in their preaching and in their living. They became great men because of their relationship to and association with the only great Man who ever lived—the great Preacher of all preachers—the Lord Jesus Christ.

The Speaking Factor (Colossians 1:28)

The fourth factor is the speaking factor. "How can they hear without someone preaching to them?" That's a rhetorical question that Paul raises in Romans 10:14. The gospel is to be communicated verbally.

John Stott has a helpful observation for us:

> Preaching is indispensable to Christianity. Without preaching a necessary part of its authenticity has been lost. For Christianity is, in its very essence, a religion of the Word of God. No attempt to understand Christianity can succeed which overlooks or denies the truth that the living God has taken the initiative to reveal himself savingly to fallen humanity; or that his self-revelation has been given by the most straightforward means of communication known to us, *namely by a word and words*; or that calls upon those who have heard his Word to speak it to others."[1] (italics mine)

The words of God are to be proclaimed through the words of men. Paul used three words to describe the speaking factor in 1:28. The first is "preach" or "proclaim" in the Greek. "Proclaim" means to proclaim as a herald. The herald always draws attention away from himself to the one he is heralding. That is what we're to do as preachers. We're to proclaim. We are to herald forth the truth about Jesus.

Jesus said, "Among those born of women there has not risen anyone greater than John the Baptist" (Matthew 11:11). John preached for probably only six months and died at age thirty, but he was a great preacher. And do you know why he was a great preacher? He was a proclaimer of Christ. When the people came to him he said, "Behold! The Lamb of God who takes away the sin of the world!" (John 1:29, NKJV). What did the people do when they heard his proclamation, when they heard his preaching? The Bible says they followed Jesus (1:36-37). That's what a preacher is to do. He is to preach Christ—not himself, not his peculiar doctrines, not his own philosophy. He is to preach Christ, and when he preaches Christ people are to hear him speak and follow Jesus. I am not to get a following. I am to instruct you so that you become followers of the Lord Jesus Christ.

The word "admonish" is another word Paul used to describe the speaking factor. "We proclaim him, *admonishing* and teaching everyone with all wisdom, so that we may present everyone perfect in Christ" (Colossians 1:28, emphasis added). The ultimate purpose for preaching and admonishing and teaching is that people be brought to perfection or spiritual maturity. Preaching should make you a better person. Preaching should feed your soul. Preaching should lift your sights. Preaching should give you encouragement to live a godly life. Preaching should be a blessing to you so that you come into a more mature relationship with Christ Jesus.

The Subject Factor (1:28)

We have already touched on the subject of our preaching. "We proclaim Him" (1:28). Every preacher of the gospel has a subject of infinite and profound dimension. I have the honor of preaching Christ, the Son of God, King of all kings, Lord of all lords, the One who flung the stars into space and created worlds out of nothing. I have the privilege of preaching this One—the only One—who can save your soul and take you to heaven. The only One who can make you a true believer, who can make you a true child of God. I have the privilege of preaching the only Person who can do all of that and infinitely more.

Paul preached Christ. Paul was obsessed with, and possessed by, the person of Jesus Christ. He was a one-subject preacher. Paul in this one chapter has presented Christ in a number of ways. He has presented Him as Deliverer (1:13), as Redeemer (1:14), as Creator (1:16), as Reconciler (1:20-21), and then he climaxes all of this with the glorious truth that Christ is our Indweller: "Christ in you, the hope of glory" (1:27).

All of those first four are objective. He is telling us *what Christ has done*. In the last one, he tells us *where Christ lives*. He comes to live in the believer. He comes to indwell us. We're not like the followers of a guru or Confucius or Buddha or Mohammed—their leaders are external. They read about their leaders on pages of their writings.

May I say to you, with the strongest possible emphasis, that our Savior and Lord is always internal; He has come to live in His people! This is the genius of the Christian Church. This is the great and glorious blessing of being a born-again Christian. We have Jesus Christ indwelling us. This was one of A.B. Simpson's favorite texts and was the inspiration for one of his greatest hymns.

> This is my wonderful story—Christ to my heart has
>   come;
> Jesus, the King of glory, finds in my heart a home.
> Christ in me, Christ in me, Christ in me—Oh,
>   wonderful story;
> Christ in me, Christ in me, Christ in me, the hope of
>   glory.[2]

The Struggling Factor (1:29)

We have the struggling factor in 1:29: "To this end I labor, struggling with all his energy, which so powerfully works in me." This verse tells us that preaching Christ is never to be a halfhearted exercise. It is labor. It is struggling. That word "struggling" was used in the context of the athletic games of Paul's day to describe an athlete giving his very best to perform—every ounce of his energy, every fiber of his being is dedicated to winning. We are to struggle like that as preachers. We are to strive to bring the truth of God to people. The labor and striving are never to be energized by mere human power, but rather it is to be work that is done by God Himself who powerfully works in me.

Is there anything worse than a boring sermon? Is there anything worse than a boring preacher, who is bored with his job, bored with the church, just waiting for retirement or a transfer? Paul was saying that the person who preaches the gospel must be a person dynamically energized by the power of the Holy Spirit. He is to labor and strive and give his best effort to the work committed to his trust.

Paul picked up this thought of spiritual struggle again in 2:1-3. He obviously carried his struggles for people beyond his direct preaching ministry. He spoke of his struggle for the saints in Colosse and Laodicea, people he had never seen face-to-face but for whom he felt a spiritual burden. This struggle undoubtedly was expressed and experienced in both the letters he wrote to them (4:16) and the prayers he offered for them (1:3). He talked to them about the Lord and then he talked to the Lord about them! This is an unbeatable combination in any ministry we have to people. Here Paul's true pastoral concern is seen.

The ultimate purpose for this struggle was that the believers in both Colosse and Laodicea might have encouraged hearts, a unity of love and the full riches of a complete understanding of the Lord Jesus Christ. He wanted them to know the illimitable treasures of wisdom and knowledge that can be found only in this glorious person. And please notice that *all* the wisdom and knowledge of God are in Him. He is God's wisdom and knowledge personified. Contrary to the false teachers, Jesus is totally sufficient. He is the eternal inexhaustible source of all God's truth. "But of Him you are in Christ Jesus, who became for us wisdom from God" (1 Corinthians 1:30, NKJV).

Questions for Reflection or Discussion

1. What six factors are essential in proclaiming or preaching the gospel?

2. How does servanthood enter into our preaching? Who is the pattern servant?

3. Why is proclaiming Christ considered by Paul to be a stewardship?

4. Is suffering for Christ negative or positive? Explain.

5. Why are words so important in ministering to the needs of people?

6. What is the supreme subject for all preachers of God's Word?

7. What were Paul's struggles all about? Are you struggling in ministry for people? How?

Endnotes

1. John R.W. Stott, *Between Two Worlds* (Grand Rapids, MI: Eerdmans, 1982), p. 15.
2. A.B. Simpson, "Christ in Me," *Hymns of the Christian Life* (Camp Hill, PA: Christian Publications, 1978), # 166.

5

Christ: Complete (Made Full) in Him

Colossians 2:4-10

I tell you this so that no one may deceive you by fine-sounding arguments. For though I am absent from you in body, I am present with you in spirit and delight to see how orderly you are and how firm your faith in Christ is.

So then, just as you received Christ Jesus as Lord, continue to live in him, rooted and built up in him, strengthened in the faith as you were taught, and overflowing with thankfulness.

See to it that no one takes you captive through hollow and deceptive philosophy, which depends on human tradition and the basic principles of this world rather than on Christ.

For in Christ all the fullness of the Deity lives in bodily form, and you have been given fullness in Christ, who is the head over every power and authority.

In the passage before us, the apostle Paul corrected the false teaching that was creeping into the church in Colosse by two great truths:

1. The Faith Principle—the answer to deceptive persuasion.
2. The Full Person—the answer to deceptive philosophy.

The Faith Principle

It is obvious from 2:4 that the Colossians were being approached by some smooth-talking and very persuasive false teachers. This is characteristic of all who teach error (Romans 16:17-18). To counteract those who came with "fine-sounding arguments" and "smooth talk," Paul did three things.

1. He focused on the fact that all *the treasures of wisdom and knowledge are hidden in Christ (2:3).* Any teaching, experience or philosophy that is added to what we have in Christ is indeed false. In Jesus we have *all.* The burden of all believers is not to add something *to* Him but rather to discover what we have *in* Him. We must plumb the depth of His person and teaching. The treasures of wisdom and knowledge in Christ are indeed hidden from the casual observer and can only be known to those who diligently seek them out!

2. Paul affirmed those who are under attack (Colossians 2:5). Although absent from the believers in Colosse, the apostle was with them in spirit. He was in fellowship with them and seeking to get their perspective and understand their needs. The distance of miles never created any distance for Paul in his relationship with the people to whom he wrote. He rejoiced to see how orderly they were and how firm they were in their faith in Christ. There was no question about them being believers. This was essential to everything that Paul would say to them as he continued his instruction.

3. He urged them to embrace the faith principle (2:6-7): "So then, just as you received Christ Jesus as Lord, continue to live [walk] in him." All the Christians in Colosse had begun their Christian lives by receiving the Lord Jesus in faith. This was primary and essential, but now they are encouraged to continue their Christian lives with the same principle of faith.

The inspired author used some very powerful words and employed some graphic imagery as he talked about how the life of believers expresses itself.

Continue to live in Him (2:6)

The KJV has "walk ye in him." The idea here has to do with the "lifestyle" we follow. Our behavior patterns, our attitudes, our day-by-day conduct are all to be in Christ. It is the same idea that the Lord Jesus gives us in John 15 regarding the Vine and the branches. Just as the branch draws life and all the fruit producing properties from the vine, so are we to abide in our Vine and take His life and bear fruit for Him.

Rooted in Him (Colossians 2:7)

" . . . continue to live in him, rooted and built up in him . . ." (2:6-7). Being rooted speaks both of our permanence and our plenty in our Savior! We are permanently secured when we send down the roots of faith with the One who is strong to keep us. And we also discover that when we are rooted in Him, He shares His very life with us. We have unlimited resources in the One who cannot fail.

Incidently, the verb form for rooted is a perfect participle which denotes a past *and* continuing action. The rooting is forever but we must recognize this on a day-to-day basis. We will never be more rooted than we are; however, we must enjoy and appropriate and experience this more and more. Jesus will never be defeated or depleted. He will never give up. He will always be infinitely able to sustain us.

Built up in Him (2:7)

"Built up" is a present participle, which teaches that we as believers *are being* built up. We are under construction as a temple for the Lord's habitation. Peter calls us "living stones" that "are being built [up] into a spiritual house" (1 Peter 2:5). In commenting on these two figures of speech, Bishop Moule says, "He is at once the deep genial soil of your life and growth and the cornerstone of your ascending structure"[1]

Strengthened in the faith (Colossians 2:7)

" . . . continue to live in him, . . . strengthened in the faith as you were taught, and overflowing with thankfulness" (2:6-7). This phrase also uses a present participle, which emphasizes continued action. It refers to a process of going on and being constantly established in the faith, in that body of truth which they had believed.

Overflowing with thankfulness (2:7)

Out of an established and constant faith they are to overflow with thanksgiving. Dr. Barclay says, "The one concern of the Christian is to tell in words and to show in life his gratitude for all that God has done for him in nature and in grace."[2] Certainly this spirit of thanksgiving will be in contrast to the secular world around us, where words of self-boasting, pride and human sufficiency abound.

This overflow of gratitude is also definitely related to the problem of the deceivers in Colosse who were attempting to move the believers away from their faith in the sufficiency of the Lord Jesus. Thanksgiving is a great spiritual preservative. Bishop Moule says concerning this:

> There is a great and profoundly reasonable power in holy thanksgiving to bring home to the soul the reality of the Treasure for which the thanks are given. The heart which looks up and blesses God for "His unspeakable Gift," His own Son, "who was delivered for our offences, raised for our justification," and glorified for our life and glory, *will develop a holy and*

*healthy instinct of rejection towards all substitutes for Him.*³ (emphasis mine)

The Full Person

The second great truth that Paul presented to the church in Colosse which is in contrast to the false "fine-sounding arguments" (2:4) and the "hollow and deceptive philosophy" (2:8) was to remind them of the One in whom all God's fullness dwells. Jesus is infinitely and eternally full and nothing can be added to Him.

The apostle said "see to it"—or as the King James says, "beware"—"that no one takes you captive" (2:8). The Colossians were to be very alert spiritually because there were those who would impose upon them a false authority and bring them into slavery. Please observe how Paul described this false teaching:

False teaching is hollow and deceptive philosophy (2:8).

All philosophy that does not teach the fullness of Christ is indeed hollow and empty. The boast of these false teachers was that their teaching would add to the Lord Jesus. They professed to have truth that would round out and make complete what the Colossians had in their inadequate faith. But the fact of the matter was that all that they offered was hollow, without substance and very deceptive.

So it is today. When we teach that the Lord Jesus is all that people need, we are often informed that this is entirely too simplistic. So added to Christ are all manner of creeds and formulas and rituals. Someone has rightly said that whatever people add to Christ will often become the distinctive doctrine of the group, will take priority and will ultimately overshadow the Lord Himself. The addition then becomes the standard by which all other belief systems or religions are judged.

False teaching depends on human tradition (2:8).

Whatever is meant by "human tradition," it is obvious that the teaching was not by divine revelation but rather by human speculation. All false religion is.

Philosophy per se is not evil. It means the "love of wisdom," and certainly all believers love and seek for true wisdom. All of us have a philosophy but it is based on divine revelation and has its focus on Him who is wisdom personified (1 Corinthians 1:30).

False teaching follows the basic principles of this world (Colossians 2:8).

Scholars don't agree about what these basic or rudimentary principles were, but they were certainly elementary in nature. Whether they were ceremonialism, washings, dietary observances or some other mystical experience, they were of the world and were totally incapable of bringing adherents into the truly deep and profound.

False teaching is not dependent on Christ (2:8).

Finally, these wrong teachings were not in any way dependent on Christ. They were not in accord with His Person or His work. They were estranged entirely from this glorious Person who is our only source and foundation. Jesus Christ is always the test and standard for all teaching. Does the doctrine agree with what the Bible teaches about Him? Does it affirm His full deity, His virgin birth, His sinless life, His infallible teaching, His atoning death and glorious resurrection? If these questions cannot be answered in the affirmative, then the teaching is wrong.

True teaching is based on the full person of Christ (2:9-10).

Paul climaxed the passage before us with one of the most profound statements on Christology to be found anywhere in the New Testament. Having corrected some of the false ideas being set forth by the deceptive teachers in Colosse, he made a magnificent statement concerning the singular superiority and supremacy of Jesus. Whereas the others taught that several traditions and certain principles were necessary, Paul said that Christ and Christ alone was all that was needed for the full and complete Christian life. "For in Christ all the fullness of the Deity lives in bodily form. . . . [Christ] is the head over every power and authority" (2:9-10).

It is clear that the apostle was moving his listeners away from any kind of religious process, principle or procedure to a *Person!* In Christ we have *all* . . . all of the fullness of Deity. You cannot have more than all of God! Trench states, "Paul is declaring that in the Son there dwells all the fullness of absolute Godhead; they were no mere rays of divine glory which gilded Him, lighting up His Person for a season and with splendour not His own; but He was, and is, absolute and perfect God."[4]

The inspired writer went on to say that this One in whom all God's fullness dwells is by virtue of this astounding fact also the "head over every power and authority" (2:10). This means that every hierarchy, whether angelic or demonic, every form of human government, every kind of authority domestic or foreign, every person in any place of power—all are under His headship. This doesn't mean that Jesus is simply at the top with a higher rank or more power. It means that He is above all rankings and has absolute power. He is apart from and over all the realm of the universe.

Previously we read, "For by him all things were created: things in heaven and on earth, visible and invisible, whether thrones or powers or rulers or authorities; all things were created by him and for him" (1:16). Jesus is therefore sovereign over all by virtue of the fact that He is the author, source and creator of all. All power flows from Him and must therefore serve His purpose.

What a great encouragement this is to us when, in secular society, we see so many prancing and posturing and proudly boasting of their power, whether political or material. Jesus is their head, whether that is acknowledged or not, and will be seen to be their head in the day of His future appearing. So we rest in His absolute rule and rejoice that no power or authority will ever usurp His sovereignty.

"You have been given fullness in Christ" (2:10). The NKJV says, "You are complete in Him." It is a staggering fact, and yet it is wonderfully true that all the fullness of the Lord Jesus has been transferred into us, His believing children. We are in Him and the fullness of God is in us!

A number of years ago there was talk about the complete man. He was to be well educated, cultured, properly trained in the social graces, an achiever in his field and a person with good friends and family. He was to contribute to those around him and have a very positive influence. In short, he was to be a well-balanced, all-around good person. Those in the behavioral sciences tell us that this complete and fully developed person will have about five qualities about him. Think with me about those qualities as we look at our text.

- *A complete person must feel loved.* Profound unhappiness comes when a person feels unloved and uncared for. The Lord Jesus has demonstrated in history His love for us in an unmistakable way. Paul showed how personal that love is when he said, "The Son of God . . . loved me and gave himself for me" (Galatians 2:20). Christ on the cross for you and me is love personified.

- *A complete person must be freed from guilt.* Guilt not dealt with is a horrendous weight on many lives. Isaiah said of Jesus, "All we like sheep have gone astray; we have turned, every one, to his own way; and the LORD has laid on Him the iniquity of us all" (Isaiah 53:6,

NKJV). Paul said, "God made him who had no sin to be sin for us, so that in him we might become the righteousness of God" (2 Corinthians 5:21).

- *A complete person will feel accepted and wanted.* The despair of rejection and the loneliness that results are more than some people can handle. In Ephesians 1:6, the apostle tells us the wonderful news that we are "accepted in the beloved [One]" (KJV). Jesus has assured us that the one who comes to Him, He will certainly not cast out (John 6:37, KJV).

- *A complete person must believe that his or her life has meaning, purpose and value.* Paul tells us that there are no unnecessary members in the Body of Christ. All have a place, a vital function and a ministry. Even the weak members are not just tolerated—they are necessary (1 Corinthians 12:22)!

- *A complete person must live in hope.* He must believe that somehow the future will be better than the present, that trials will pass and that things will improve. Only in Christ do we have the absolute certainty that the future will be bright and beautiful. Titus 2:13 tells us that we look for "the blessed hope—the glorious appearing of our great God and Savior, Jesus Christ."

Yes, we are complete and have all fullness in Christ. In an empty and barren world and in my personal spiritual bankruptcy, I can find Christ gloriously, perfectly and eternally adequate.

Questions for Reflection or Discussion

1. Describe the false teachers in Colosse. How were the believers to deal with them?

2. What caused Paul to rejoice as he wrote to the church in Colosse?

3. What are the five ways a believer is to live his life and express his faith as given in Colossians 2:6 and 7?

4. Does the giving of thanks have anything to do with us being preserved from false teaching? Explain.

5. Give the characteristics of deceptive philosophy.

6. Discuss what it means to experience the fullness of Jesus Christ.

Endnotes

1. H.C.G. Moule, *Colossian Studies* (New York: D.D. Hodder and Stoughton, 1898), p. 129.
2. William Barclay, *The Letters to the Philippians, Colossians, and Thessalonians*, Daily Bible Studies (Toronto, ON: Welch Co., 1956), p. 132.
3. Moule, p. 130.
4. R.C. Trench, quoted in Werest, *Word Studies in the Greek New Testament* (Grand Rapids, MI: Eerdmans, 1953), p. 203.

6

Christ: Delivered in Him

Colossians 2:11-15

In him you were also circumcised, in the putting off of the sinful nature, not with a circumcision done by the hands of men but with the circumcision done by Christ, having been buried with him in baptism and raised with him through your faith in the power of God, who raised him from the dead.

When you were dead in your sins and in the uncircumcision of your sinful nature, God made you alive with Christ. He forgave us all our sins, having canceled the written code, with its regulations, that was against us and that stood opposed to us; he took it away, nailing it to the cross. And having disarmed the powers and authorities, he made a public spectacle of them, triumphing over them by the cross.

What a glorious passage of Scripture about the deliverance of God's people by the Lord Jesus Christ the great Deliverer. Our text indicates that we have been delivered in four ways: He has delivered us from our sinful nature; He has delivered us from spiritual death; He has delivered us from legal regulations; and He has delivered us from satanic authority. The Lord is the great Deliverer.

He Has Delivered Us from Our Sinful Nature

To show how the Lord delivers us from our sinful nature, Paul spoke about circumcision. In contrast to Old Testament circumcision, Paul taught that New Testament circumcision is three things:

Divine, not human (2:11)

"In him [Jesus] you were also circumcised" (2:11). Paul spoke of the circumcision of Christ. In the Old Testament, a priest, a mortal human being, would circumcise the little Jewish boys. That circumcision was a sign of their covenant relationship. It was to indicate that they belonged to Abraham and his family. When we come to the New Testament, we discover that a priest doesn't circumcise us physically, but rather the great High Priest Jesus Christ circumcises us spiritually.

Spiritual, not physical (2:11-12)

We read it is circumcision made without hands. It is spiritual surgery that only the Master Surgeon, Jesus Christ, can perform. He performed this spiritual surgery when we trusted Him as our Savior.

The removal, the putting off, the casting away of the fleshly nature (2:12)

It is not the removal of a small piece of flesh from the body. The old nature I received from my father Adam has been put away by the Lord Jesus—not eradicated, but put away. This Jesus Christ not only died for my sins (plural), but He also died to deliver me from my sin nature—that which causes me to sin, that which is deep within me and lusts and hates and is greedy and selfish, that nature within me that expresses itself in the sins of the flesh. That sin nature was put away by the spiritual circumcision of the Lord Jesus Christ.

This sinful nature is referred to in different ways in the Bible. It is called the carnal mind (Romans 8:6, KJV), the old man (Romans 6:6 and Colossians 3:9, KJV) and the natural man (1 Corinthians 2:14, KJV). That old nature has already been dealt with by the Lord Jesus Christ. Most of us are dealing with sins and are concerned with habits and the manifestation of evil in our lives. What we really should do is get at the source, the root, the cause. Christ has already gotten to that source, root and cause. He has, by spiritual circumcision, put that away from us. We must recognize this by faith and live in the reality of it day by day.

What Jesus put away historically and actually at the cross, we are to put away experientially and personally through our entire spiritual journey.

It should be pointed out that there was a strong spiritual dimension to circumcision in the Old Testament as well. Those who really understood the deeper meaning of circumcision knew that it was far more than the removal of the foreskin of their baby sons. For example, they spoke of uncircumcised *lips* (Exodus 6:12, KJV), uncircumcised *hearts* (Ezekiel 44:9) and uncircumcised *ears* (Jeremiah 6:10, KJV). Obviously, God's covenant people were to have more than just the sign of that covenant; they were to have a deep relationship with the God of that covenant.

Now we move to the second thought. The Lord has not only delivered us from our sinful nature, He has delivered us from spiritual death.

He Has Delivered Us from Our Spiritual Death

In Colossians 2:12-13 Paul spoke of three kinds of death.

Spiritual death (2:13)

There is spiritual death for all people who are outside of Christ. This is what Paul meant when he wrote, "dead in your sins" (2:13). Paul said the same thing in Ephesians 2:5, "dead in transgressions."

Being spiritually dead means being *devoid of the life of God.* It means that I have only human life. I do not have His life. I have only the life and the nature that I received from my father Adam who was marked for death the day he rebelled against heaven. I have received from him mortal life, but only through Christ do I receive *eternal* life, immortal life. Only through Christ do I receive the very life of God. "He who has the Son has life; he who does not have the Son of God does not have life" (1 John 5:12). We are spiritually dead until we receive the Son of life, the Son of God. At the moment when I receive Jesus Christ into my life, I come alive to God; I receive eternal life, the very life of God Himself. As long as God lives I will live because of the presence of Jesus Christ in me. It is a marvelous thing to possess the eternal life that is found in Jesus Christ.

This spiritual death also means to be *separated from God.* To be spiritually dead is to be separated from God. You will recall when the Lord spoke to Adam He said, "When you eat of [the forbidden fruit] you will surely die" (Genesis 2:17). Adam ate of the forbidden fruit but kept right on living. His heart kept right on beating. His respiration was strong and all the vital signs were there. But he died immediately spiritually. He died to God. God went looking for him in the garden, but the fellowship they had once enjoyed was now gone. There was separation because of sin.

All of us are born in this separated condition, and if we do not trust Christ to bring us to God, we will die and experience what the Bible calls "the second death." We will be separated from God forever.

To be spiritually dead means also to be *totally helpless.* A dead person cannot do anything to change his condition. He must receive life from outside himself. Only Jesus can reach into the darkness of the grave of spiritually dead people and say, as He did to Lazarus, "Come forth" (John 11:43, KJV). Jesus must take the initiative and speak the living word or else people will remain forever dead and separated from God.

Death of Christ (Colossians 2:12, 14)

The second kind of death we see in our passage is the death of Christ. The cross is mentioned in Colossians 2:14 and God raising Him from the dead in 2:12. "Christ died for our sins" the Bible says (1 Corinthians 15:3). He was put on the cross in our place. He was punished that I might not be punished. He was condemned that I might not be condemned. He suffered vicariously. He was enveloped in darkness when He hung on the cross and cried out, "My God, my God, why have you forsaken me?" (Mark 15:34). He did all of that in order to save you and me.

Death of believers with Christ (Colossians 2:12)

Then we have the death of believers with Christ. Colossians 2:12 says, "buried with him . . . raised with him." Paul was saying, historically, "You were there when Jesus died and you died in Him. You were there when Jesus was buried and you were buried in Him. You were there when Jesus was raised from the dead and you were raised in Him." We have died with Christ. We have been buried with Christ. We have been raised up to walk in newness of life with the Lord Jesus.

In Galatians 5:24 Paul said, "Those who belong to Christ Jesus have crucified the sinful nature with its passions and desires" and in 2:20: "I have been crucified with Christ and I no longer live, but Christ lives in me." Paul was saying that the old man, the old nature, the old self, went to the cross when Jesus went to the cross. I died in Him—my old nature was crucified. I was buried with Him and I was raised with Him in resurrection power. This of course was done historically and positionally for all of God's children.

Look at Romans 6:1-8, 11.

> What shall we say, then? Shall we go on sinning so that grace may increase? By no means! We died to sin; how can we live in it any longer? Or don't you know that all of us who were baptized into Christ Jesus were baptized into his death? We were therefore buried with him through baptism into death in order that, just as Christ was raised from the dead through the glory of the Father, we too may live a new life.
>
> If we have been united with him like this in his death, we will certainly also be united with him in his resurrection. For we know that our old self was crucified with him so that the body of sin might be done away with, that we should no longer be slaves to sin—because anyone who has died has been freed from sin.
>
> Now if we died with Christ, we believe that we will also live with him. . . .
>
> In the same way, count yourselves dead to sin but alive to God in Christ Jesus.

The Lord Jesus Christ didn't just die for our sins. We died in Him. Now we are to reckon, or count, this to be true. Paul always stated a fact before he made an application, and he did it here. Make application of it to your life. Live every day with these thoughts: *I have been crucified. The old self, the ugly me, the lustful me, the proud me, the selfish me, has been crucified with Christ. In addition to this, I have been raised to walk in resurrection power. I have been raised to walk in the life of Jesus Christ. That is the dynamism of the Christian life. That gives me energy. That gives me strength. That gives me power to know and do the will of God and be a holy person.*

Some of us have the idea that God reconditioned the old nature. He didn't recondition it, renovate it, regenerate it, reconstruct it, reeducate it, repress it or renew it. The old nature was so totally and so absolutely without any redeemable qualities that He crucified it. Paul said in Romans 8:7 that the carnal mind "is hostile to God. It does not submit to God's law, nor can it do so." If you are expecting anything out of the old nature to please God, my friend, you are on the wrong track. The old nature will never please God. That is why it was crucified. That is why it was nailed to the cross. Let's leave it there. Wouldn't it be wonderful if all of us would leave our old nature on the cross?

The Christian life isn't trying to do a little better. It isn't trying to be religious or coming under some regulations and rules and trying somehow through that to become better people. The Christian life is taking my life to the cross, *dying*, taking Jesus' life out of an empty tomb and *living!* That's the Christian life. This is the essential secret of the Christian life.

He Has Delivered Us from Legal Regulations (2:14)

The Lord Jesus has delivered us from legal regulations, "having wiped out [erased permanently, canceled] the handwriting of requirements that was against us" (2:14, NKJV). This is referring to the law of Moses. Moses' law was against us, contrary to us.

Now before you draw any wrong conclusions, let me say that the law in itself was good. When we think of the moral code, when we think of the Ten Commandments, remember that God is the author and giver of the law. It is an expression of His own character. It is the highest form of stated moral conduct that has ever been written. There is nothing wrong with the law of God, but there is a lot wrong with me—and that is where the problem comes in. Paul said, "In my inner being I delight in God's law" (Romans 7:22). It was good because it reflected the Lord. But the law was bad because it revealed our sin and condemned us and yet was powerless to take our sin away. No one is ever saved by the law. No one is ever forgiven one single sin through keeping the law. The law never delivered anyone or made anyone holy. No one is ever brought into a relationship to God through the law.

The law is against us because the law is perfect and we are sinful. The law speaks of that which is right, and we are wrong. The law speaks of good, and we are bad. The law is light, and we are darkness. Paul said it succinctly in Romans 3:19-20, "Now we know that whatever the law says, it says to those who are under the law, so that every mouth may be silenced and the whole world held accountable to God. Therefore no one will be declared righteous in his sight by observing the law; rather, through the law we become conscious of sin." Galatians 3:10 has something to say along the same lines. "For as many as are of the works of the law are under the curse; for it is written, 'Cursed is everyone who does not continue in all things which are written in the book of the law, to do them' " (NKJV). That is heavy stuff. That says that I am cursed by the law that I have broken. The law condemns me because I haven't kept it.

However, there is good news. Galatians 3:13 says, "Christ has redeemed us from the curse of the law, having become a curse for us (for it is written, 'Cursed is everyone who hangs on a tree')" (NKJV). The law doesn't curse me, a believer. It has already cursed my Savior. I am not cursed by the law because Jesus took the curse of that law when He died for you and me. Every single transgression of the law was laid on Jesus. He suffered for all the sin, of all people, of all time. Thus these regulations, these laws, have been wiped out. They have been canceled (Colossians 2:14). God nailed it all to His Son's cross.

Our indictment was crucified with Jesus. We must not go back to that old law and try to find forgiveness or help or blessing or encouragement from it. It will not bring release; it will bring only bondage.

He Has Delivered Us from Satanic Authority (2:15)

Finally we have been delivered from satanic authority. Jesus, "having disarmed principalities and powers, He made a public spectacle of them, triumphing over them in it" (2:15, NKJV). Another deliverance that the Lord Jesus accomplished on the cross for all believers is our deliverance from the power and authority of Satan and all his demonic forces. Jesus has disarmed and stripped our enemy of all his weapons. Whatever Satan was bringing against the people of God, whatever destructive forces he was using to destroy the people of God, they have been taken away. The Lord has disarmed him. And then Jesus has made Satan and all of his cohorts a public spectacle. He has openly conquered our enemy through the cross and the resurrection. "Since the children have flesh and blood, he too shared in their humanity so that by his death he might destroy him who holds the power of death—that is, the devil—and free those who all their lives were held in slavery by their fear of death" (Hebrews 2:14-15).

Through death Jesus has destroyed him who has the power of death, the devil. It doesn't say he annihilated him—He has destroyed him. He has annulled his power and authority. He has broken him at the cross. Satan no longer has any authority over you as a believer. "We are more than conquerors through him who loved us," the Bible says (Romans 8:37). A triumph is a celebration of a conquest. You never triumph on the battlefield—you fight on the battlefield. You defeat your enemy on the battlefield; then, when you get off the battlefield, you triumph. We are following the Lord Jesus who has already destroyed the enemy. He has already conquered Satan and all of his cohorts. We follow Him now in triumph. We follow Him and celebrate the victory.

Let me quote from Dr. Barclay:

> One other great picture flashes on the screen of Paul's mind. Jesus has stripped the powers and authorities and made them His captives. As we have seen, the ancient world believed in all kinds of angels and all kinds of elemental spirits. Many of these spirits were out to ruin men. It was they who were responsible for demon possession and the like. They were hostile to men. Jesus conquered them forever. He stripped them. The word used is the word for stripping the weapons and the armour from a defeated foe. Once and for all Jesus broke their power. He put them to open shame and led them captive in His triumphant train. The picture is that of the triumph of a Roman general. When a Roman general had won a really notable victory he was allowed to march his victorious armies through the streets of Rome and behind him followed the kings and the leaders and peoples he had vanquished. They were openly branded as his spoils. Paul thinks of Jesus as the Conqueror enjoying a kind of cosmic triumph and in His triumphal procession are the powers of evil, beaten forever for everyone to see.[1]

So, beloved believers, you and I have been delivered from these powers. The Lord Jesus has conquered the enemy. We follow in the train of His triumph. It is a wonderful thing to have a triumphant Savior. There aren't too many triumphs anymore. There are a lot of defeats in this world, a lot of businesses going down, a lot of people going down, a lot of governments going down, a lot of nations going down. In a world of defeat and darkness and destruction, we are following a winner. We celebrate the victory and rejoice in our deliverance.

All of this reminds us again that we believers are a Christ-centered people. Eight different references are made in our Scripture portion to Christ and His work. Deliverance does not come from any human ability or self effort, as well intentioned as they might be.

God give us grace then to stop trying and struggling and begin trusting—simply and solely trusting the only One who cannot fail . . . the One who is always a winner!

> Jesus, what a strength in weakness!
>   Let me hide myself in Him;
> Tempted, tried, and sometimes failing,
>   He, my strength, my victory wins.
>
> Hallelujah! What a Saviour!
>   Hallelujah! What a friend!
> Saving, helping, keeping, loving,
>   He is with me to the end.[2]

Questions for Reflection or Discussion

1. What are the three features of New Testament circumcision?

2. What three kinds of death does Paul speak of in our Scripture portion? How are these meaningful to you?

3. Why is the resurrection so essential in the Christian life?

4. What has the Lord done with the written code (the law) and its regulations in relation to the believer?

5. How are these regulations against us?

6. Where did Jesus "disarm" the powers and authorities of Satan? How?

7. Are the terms "conquer" and "triumph" the same? Explain.

Endnotes

1. William Barclay, *The Letters to the Philippians, Colossians, and Thessalonians,* Daily Bible Studies (Toronto, ON: Welch Co., 1956), p. 143.
2. J. Wilbur Chapman, "Our Great Saviour," *Hymns of the Christian Life* (Camp Hill, PA: Christian Publications, 1978), # 335.

7

Christ: Free in Him

Colossians 2:16-23

Therefore do not let anyone judge you by what you eat or drink, or with regard to a religious festival, a New Moon celebration or a Sabbath day. These are a shadow of the things that were to come; the reality, however, is found in Christ. Do not let anyone who delights in false humility and the worship of angels disqualify you for the prize. Such a person goes into great detail about what he has seen, and his unspiritual mind puffs him up with idle notions. He has lost connection with the Head, from whom the whole body, supported and held together by its ligaments and sinews, grows as God causes it to grow.

Since you died with Christ to the basic principles of this world, why, as though you still belonged to it, do you submit to its rules: "Do not handle! Do not taste! Do not touch!"? These are all destined to perish with use, because they are based on human commands and teachings. Such regulations indeed have an appearance of wisdom, with their self-imposed worship, their false humility and their harsh treatment of the body, but they lack any value in restraining sensual indulgence.

Let freedom ring from the snow-capped Rockies of Colorado!

Let freedom ring from the curvaceous peaks of California!

But' not only that; let freedom ring from Stone Mountain of Georgia!

Let freedom ring from Lookout Mountain of Tennessee!

Let freedom ring from every hill and mole hill of Mississippi!

From every mountainside, let freedom ring!

When we let freedom ring, when we let it ring from every village and every hamlet, from every state and every city, we will be able to speed up that day when all God's children—black men and white men, Jews and Gentiles, Protestants and Catholics—will be able to join hands and sing in the words of the old Negro spiritual, "Free at last! Free at last! Thank God Almighty, we are free at last!"[1]

These impassioned words were the dramatic climax of an address given by Dr. Martin Luther King, Jr. from the steps of the Lincoln Memorial in Washington, D.C. in 1963. One doesn't have to agree with all that Dr. King said or did to understand that the supreme passion of his life was to see black people set free from the bondage of racial, social and political injustice. He wanted freedom no matter how costly. He seemed to feel that freedom was the most important thing in life.

As we look at our world, we see bondage manifesting itself not only in injustice, but also in many other ways. We are an addiction-prone society. We are controlled by anger, alcohol, promiscuous lifestyles, pleasure, pride, possession and even the maddening master of an impossible work schedule.

There is, however, another kind of bondage that the apostle addresses in the Scripture before us. It is not as obvious or as ugly in appearance as other forms of bondage, but it is a terrible bondage nonetheless, and it has profound eternal consequences. It is religious bondage.

There were people infiltrating the Colossian congregation with religious teachings that promised to add spiritual value to the believers, but which were in fact threatening to take away their freedom and impose regulations and religious experiences in conflict with the absolute sufficiency of the Person and work of Christ.

We will look at two things as Paul instructed us by the Spirit:

1. The False Religious Practices Identified.
2. The False Religious Practices Rejected.

The Religious Practices Identified (2:16)

There were three different kinds of religious practices creeping into the church: asceticism, mysticism and legalism. All of these "isms" were to be in addition to the Lord Jesus. The advocates of these practices were saying you need more than Jesus—you need these spiritual "enhancers."

Asceticism

Asceticism is the teaching that through self-torture or self-denial one can discipline oneself to reach a higher spiritual or intellectual state. These teachers were saying that it's not enough that you have Jesus Christ. You must also put yourself under some rigid rules. You must not eat or drink certain things. You must indeed have a very strong hand upon yourself. You must induce suffering because only through this will you really enter into a deep experience.

Notice in Colossians 2:21 that Paul actually quoted these folks: "Do not handle! Do not taste! Do not touch!" In 2:23 he spoke about these people teaching a harsh treatment of the body. In the Christian Church we have always had people who practiced and taught asceticism. During the middle ages monasticism became popular. There were monasteries put up all over the world, and people went there and took vows of celibacy and poverty. They had long fasts when they didn't eat or drink. They slept on hard beds with only one blanket. They crawled upstairs on their knees—hoping through all of this to mortify the body to put down sinful desire and to become holy people. The problem was, they discovered, that each one of them took their unholy hearts and their unholy desires and their unholy natures right inside the monastery walls. Going away somewhere, buffeting your body, refusing to eat, practicing all kinds of self-mortification will never bring you the deeper life. It will bring you a narrow, enslaved kind of existence that will take the joy of living and will put you in great bondage.

I must say that in some of those monasteries there were people who discovered the secret of Jesus Christ and entered into a real relationship with Him in spite of the rules. You see, God overrules men's rules and some of the bad things we do in religion.

Mysticism

Mysticism is the philosophy that the direct knowledge of God or spiritual truth is attainable through intuition, insight, visions or in a way differing from ordinary sense perception. It tends to put subjective experience above objective truth. People that are into mysticism don't ask the question, "What is the truth?" Their question is, "What is your experience?" Experience is the most important thing with mystics.

A good kind of mysticism does exist. I think I'm something of a mystic. I do experience the presence of God when I worship Him. I do hear the voice of the Holy Spirit when I read the Word of God. I do celebrate His goodness when I pray and praise. I do enjoy an awareness that the Lord is with me, that He is ordering my steps and directing my paths, that my life is in His hands and that my times are under His providential control.

The kind of mysticism that was coming into the church at Colosse was different. It was moving people away from Jesus. The center of their experience was not in Him but in all kinds of experiences they had of an emotional and psychological nature (2:18).

Legalism

This is the doctrine that, in addition to Christ and His work, a believer must keep some of the requirements of the Old Testament law in order to attain full spiritual life. The legalist followed Paul everywhere he went. Paul preached Christ *period.* The legalist preached Christ *plus*: plus circumcision, plus dietary laws, plus ordinances, plus Sabbath keeping, plus the new moon, plus the festival seasons—plus, plus, plus. Jesus Christ *period* is what Paul preached. If ever a book had as its theme that statement—Jesus Christ *period*—it is the book of Colossians. Christ is all and in all.

The point is that legalists put a heavy burden on the people and they said, "Unless you do these things, unless you stop doing these things, you will never enter into a full Christian life." That is legalism. So how did Paul deal with these false ideas?

The Religious Practices Rejected

Paul said that every believer should have a strong resistance in his life to the people who come and say that Jesus is not enough. "Therefore do not let anyone judge you by what you eat or drink" (2:16). In other words, don't let anyone put you in some dietary restriction. Paul went on to add that believers should not let anyone "disqualify [them] for the prize" (2:18). Don't let anyone take your reward away from you by leading you astray. In both of these statements it is abundantly clear that all the believers in Colosse were to stand against and reject all who would impose upon them teaching that was contrary to Jesus and His sufficiency. Let me suggest five ways by which we reject false religious ideas.

1. Distinguish between the shadows of the Old Testament and the reality of Christ (2:17).

We reject false religious ideas by distinguishing between the shadows, or symbols, of the Old Testament and the substance, or reality, of Christ in the New Testament. The shadow is always inferior to the substance that casts the shadow. The Old Testament is full of shadows of the Lord Jesus: in the tabernacle, in the sacrificial system, in the feast days, in the priesthood and in the prophecies that the prophets gave concerning Him. But remember, those are shadows. They are looking forward to Christ. We don't go back to shadows; we embrace the substance and the reality of Jesus today.

The type is inferior to the antitype. The Old Testament ceremony is inferior to that Person whom that ceremony pictures. There were many lambs in the Old Testament. They couldn't take away sin. That is why they kept sacrificing lambs—lamb after lamb after lamb. Then one day Jesus came. What did John the Baptist say? "Behold, another lamb"? No. He said, "Behold *the* Lamb of God, which taketh away the sin of the world" (John 1:29, KJV, emphasis added).

The prophecy is inferior to the fulfillment. If we go back to the shadows we are regressing, not progressing. These false teachers said, "You want to progress in your Christian life? Then get circumcised. Be careful about your dietary laws. Keep the Sabbath." And on and on it went. This was regression, not progression. This was shadow, not substance.

2. Distinguish between self-centered experience and Christ-centered faith (Colossians 2:18-19).

"Do not let anyone who delights in false humility and the worship of angels disqualify you for the prize. Such a person goes into great detail about what he has seen, and his unspiritual mind puffs him up with idle notions" (2:18). These people were apparently worshiping angels and were very proud of their "superior" experience. Again, we must distinguish between self-centered experience and Christ-centered faith. It is very easy to have false humility and be puffed up with pride when you focus on your experience. Remember, we do not come to Truth through experience. We come to experience through Truth. When you experience the Truth, that Truth will set you free, and He will nourish your soul and He will bless you, comfort you and invigorate you. It is the Truth who sets us free, not our mystical experience.

3. Distinguish between living under and dying to the law (2:20-21).

We reject false religious ideas by distinguishing between living under the law and dying to the law. Paul spoke about the law, as it was being used by these false teachers, as principles of the world (2:20)—not the Word. These worldly principles were the secular approach from the secular mind. He spoke of them as regulations—"do not" is used three times. "Do not handle! Do not taste! Do not touch!" (2:21). Is the Christian life a list of "do nots"? No, the Christian life is not a negative religion. The Christian life is Christ, Christ alive in me. That is the most positive, invigorating, life-blessing, happy experience that anyone can have.

Rules, in the religious meaning of the word, will never set you free. Rules will bring you into bondage. Paul said that we are not living under the law; we have died to the law. This is stated clearly in 2:20: "Since you died with Christ to the basic principles of this world, why, as though you still belonged to it, do you submit to its rules?" A rule, a commandment, a man-made ordinance, cannot control or rule over a person who is dead. Death has taken that man out from under any influence or effect the rule might have on him. Have you ever seen a corpse keep rules? A corpse just lies there, totally unresponsive to any external stimuli, totally unresponsive to any rules. You can't talk to a corpse and say, "You must keep the law." He will just lie there in cold death and stare back at you and not say one thing.

Paul said repeatedly in this chapter that we have died to the law in Christ. "Having canceled the written code, with its regulations, that was against us and that stood opposed to us; he took it away, nailing it to the cross" (2:14).

4. Distinguish between experience in isolation and edification in the congregation (2:19).

Mystics are always in isolation, having a very personal experience that is apart from others. Some in the Colossian assembly were having these experiences, and what were the results? "Such a person goes into great detail about what he has seen, and his unspiritual mind puffs him up with idle notions" (2:18).

These people were so into their experiences that nothing else mattered. The mystical experience took priority over everything and everyone else, and especially the Lord Jesus Christ. And as we have already seen, this led to feelings of pride and a sense of superiority over others in the congregation who had not had the same experience.

The person who does this, Paul said, "has lost connection with the Head, from whom the whole body, supported and held together by its ligaments and sinews, grows as God causes it to grow" (2:19). When I make mysticism supreme, I lose my connection with the Lord Jesus, the Head of the body. It is tragic when I value an experience over the Sovereign Head of the Church!

Another enormous problem to the false mystic is that when he isolates himself from the body of Christ, he loses the "togetherness" and support that the Lord Jesus provides for His own within the fellowship of that body. The NKJV says that we are "nourished and knit together" and that *"all the body* [not just isolated members] . . . grows with the increase that is from God"* (2:19, emphasis mine).

There is a mutual dependence within the body of Christ on the Lord Jesus for growth and spiritual development. At the same time there is an interdependence on one another because the Lord works through all the members of His body to bring about this growth. We need Him and we need one another.

5. Distinguish between the harsh treatment of the physical body and the health of the spiritual body (2:22-23).

Finally, we reject false religious ideas by distinguishing between the harsh treatment of the physical body and the health, vigor and growth of the spiritual body of Christ. Paul clearly taught that the harsh treatment of our bodies can never restrain us from sensual indulgence (2:23). Self can never tame self. Self can never create holiness. There is never a physical cure for a spiritual or moral ill.

We must remember that the Lord Jesus, as the Head of His body, never represses or severely restricts the members within His body. Rather, He always gives us the vitality of His all-powerful life and thus enables us to grow strong and function freely as we carry out His will.

When we as members are open and submissive to the Head, then we shall know the profound meaning of our Lord's words, "If the Son sets you free, you will be free indeed" (John 8:36). Yes, *free indeed!*

Questions for Reflection or Discussion

1. Give the three false religious practices that were being brought into the Colossian church. Explain the teaching of each.

2. Do you see these teachings in the religious world today? If so, give examples.

3. How were the believers in Colosse to respond to those who were trying to impose regulations on them?

4. Why are the "shadows" of the Old Testament inferior to the "reality" or "substance" of the New Testament?

5. Discuss the statement: "We do not come to Truth through experience; we come to experience through Truth."

6. Two kinds of bodies are mentioned in our text at 2:19 and 23. Define them and explain how they are important to Paul's teaching on spiritual freedom.

Endnote

1. Martin Luther King, Jr. in Lewis Copeland and Lawrence W. Lamm, *The World's Great Speeches* (New York: Dover Publications, 1973), p. 754.

Part 2

The Sanctification and Service of the People of Christ

(Practical)

8

Christ: All in All

Colossians 3:1-11

Since, then, you have been raised with Christ, set your hearts on things above, where Christ is seated at the right hand of God. Set your minds on things above, not on earthly things. For you died, and your life is now hidden with Christ in God. When Christ, who is your life, appears, then you also will appear with him in glory.

Put to death, therefore, whatever belongs to your earthly nature: sexual immorality, impurity, lust, evil desires and greed, which is idolatry. Because of these, the wrath of God is coming. You used to walk in these ways, in the life you once lived. But now you must rid yourselves of all such things as these: anger, rage, malice, slander, and filthy language from your lips. Do not lie to each other, since you have taken off your old self with its practices and have put on the new self, which is being renewed in knowledge in the image of its Creator. Here there is no Greek or Jew, circumcised or uncircumcised, barbarian, Scythian, slave or free, but Christ is all, and is in all.

You will observe that we are entering into a different division of the book of Colossians. We had in the first two chapters "The Supremacy and Sufficiency of the Person of

Christ." In the last two chapters we have "The Sanctification and Service of the People of Christ." This book divides neatly in the middle, as many of Paul's epistles do.

In the first part you have the theological and in the last part you have the practical. He not only sets forth great truths about the Lord Jesus Christ in Colossians in chapters 1 and 2 but he shows the application of those great truths in chapters 3 and 4. The Bible is a practical book. It is not only a book that gives us theological knowledge, it is a book that ministers to our souls—nurturing, instructing, convicting, correcting, comforting, helping. It ministers to every need that we have.

It is always important that when we embrace the truth of God's Word we say to the Holy Spirit who offers the truth, "Gracious Spirit, help me to live this truth out. Help me to apply it. Help me to absorb it. Help me to understand it. Help me to love it. Help me to know it. Help me to reflect it in the way I live, in my attitudes, in my actions, in my reactions."

Our text gives us one of the most profound portions in the New Testament. In fact, the first four verses of this chapter have to be some of the greatest verses that ever flowed from the inspired apostle's pen. He is taking us here into spiritual realms of immense and enormous dimensions. But even though we have truth here that we undoubtedly will be looking at and seeking to learn even in heaven, it does have practical meaning to me now. It speaks to my condition. It can indeed change my life. It can give me a new perspective. It can give me a new spiritual energy. It can give me the ability to do the will of God and to please Him in this world. Let us not only plumb its depth but also experience its practicality as well.

In the passage we discover that the believer has life in four dimensions: life above, life below, life within, life beyond. That is all to life there is.

The Believer Has Life Above (3:1-4)

The believer does indeed have life above. Paul says, "Set your hearts on things above" (3:1).

The secularist and the modern humanist do not believe that there is life above. They live their lives in what philosophers call "a closed system." All that they have is in themselves and their environment. They are limited to their resources and abilities. God is ruled out. Angels are ruled out. Heaven is ruled out. Truth beyond what we can pragmatically discover in our work place, in our schools or in our institutions is ruled out.

But the greatest thing you and I have today is not here below; it is up above. We must live life as believers with a heavenly perspective. Whatever I set my heart on, whatever I set my mind on, controls my life. Paul was saying this is how the Christian life is to be lived. This is how I am to be controlled. This is the realm in which I am to serve the Lord. I am to set my mind on things above. I am to live in the reality of the spiritual world. I am to live in the reality of the world that is beyond my senses, beyond the laboratories, beyond the university classroom, beyond the scholars' intellect. I am to seek, as the passion and focus and direction of my life, the things which are above.

Are you a seeker of things above? Do you set your mind every day to think thoughts after Jesus, to set your mind on Him who sits at the Father's right hand? That is the question we need to answer. The believer has life above.

There is a fascinating progression in what the apostle says to us in regard to our relationship with Christ. Think with me carefully about this progression because it is very important. He says that we have died with Christ (2:20), we have been buried with Christ (2:12), we have been raised with Christ (2:12; 3:1) and finally he teaches us that we have ascended with Christ (3:1). Our focus then is not on the cross. Our focus is not on the tomb. Our focus is not on Jesus out of the tomb, walking the dusty roads of Galilee in His post-resurrection ministry, as essential as these all are. Our focus is on His ascension and His exalted position at the Father's right hand!

We look at Jesus on the throne. That is where He is now. This is the ultimate in the experience of Jesus Christ. He finished His earthly work and now sits as our great High Priest to do His heavenly work. There was no chair in the tabernacle and there was no chair in the temple. Why was there no furniture for the priests to sit on? Because the priest's work was never done. It was one sacrificial lamb after another. It was not until the Lamb of God came that the work was finished. When Jesus, God's lamb, died on the cross, that was the sacrifice to end all sacrifices. His last words were, "It is finished" (John 19:30). He then went back and sat down at the right hand of God Almighty (Hebrews 1:3).

The ultimate in the believer's life with the Lord is to move with Him through these experiences: crucified with Him, buried with Him, raised with Him and ascended with Him. We must move by faith to our *above* position in Christ, because that is where we are. We are "hidden with Christ in God" (Colossians 3:3). We are to seek those things that are "above, where Christ is" (3:1). In other words, our focus is not so much on a location as it is on a *Person.* He is above. He is seated on the throne at His Father's right hand. Therefore, we seek Him. Our focus is not on a crucified Jesus or an entombed Jesus but rather on an enthroned Jesus. We seek Him.

> Go up, reluctant heart,
>   Take up thy rest above;
> Arise, earth-clinging thoughts;
>   Ascend, my lingering love.[1]

We see three things in the enthroned Lord. We have *sovereignty,* we have *sufficiency* and we have *security.*

Sovereignty

Christ is sitting at the Father's right hand. The ultimate purpose of God in redemption was to bring His Son back to heaven and give Him the throne. It pleased the Father to do that and Jesus today is sitting on the throne of grace and glory.

After cruel men spat in His face, beat His body, drove nails through His hands and feet and blasphemed His holy name—after men did their worst, God did His best. He took His Son out of their hands. He took His Son back to heaven and gave Him the throne of the universe.

We are not trusting a loser. We are trusting a winner. We are trusting one who succeeded, marvelously, wonderfully and supernaturally. His mission is accomplished and King Jesus sits on the throne.

He is above all principalities and powers. He is above all the rulers, all of the circumstances, all of the forces, all of the darkness, all of the political and military intrigue, all of the chaos of this world. Jesus Christ is above all.

There is a wonderfully elevating thing about all of this: we are there with Him. "But God, who is rich in mercy, because of His great love with which He loved us, even when we were dead in trespasses, made us alive together with Christ (by grace you have been saved), and raised us up together, and made us sit together in the heavenly places in Christ Jesus" (Ephesians 2:4-6, NKJV). We share the throne with King Jesus! We sit in heavenly realms.

Just as the Lord is above all that is in this world, we sit above all that is in this world. We are not slaves, not under any regulation, force or personality. It means that we are totally free in Jesus Christ. We are free to reign over all the things that we encounter. We are not to be under the oppression, the defeat, the discouragement of this world. We are to live a life that is above all of that. Sometimes people answer the question, "How are things?" by responding, "Well, pretty well *under the circumstances.*"

What a horrible place to be—under the circumstances! Some of you are without employment, some of you are struggling in your business like you have never struggled before, some of you have family problems that won't end, some of you are lonely and discouraged. In Christ you are above all of your problems. In Christ you are above all of your sicknesses. In Christ you are above your company. In Christ you are above your unemployment. In Christ you are above your weaknesses. In Christ you are above your failures. In Christ you are above all of those forces that would bring you down, that would wring the joy of life out of you and make you a limp, defeated rag.

In Christ Jesus we are seated in heaven. Does that make a difference in the way we live on earth? It surely does. There is no influence in this world that can control us to the point of taking us out of the will of God. There is no influence in this world that can control us by depressing us and bring us down to defeat. There is no force stronger than the sovereign power of the enthroned King. He has overcome, already, everything that we will ever face. We are sitting in King Jesus above all that is here below.

We embrace this truth whether we fully understand it or see clearly all its application or not. We must embrace it with the prayer, "Lord Jesus, teach me what it means to be seated with You on the throne of glory. Teach me what it means to be above my problems, to be above my difficulties, to be above my circumstances, to be above my temptations. Teach me what it means, Lord. I want to know my throne rights. I want to know what it means to be a person who is above all that this world is or can do." The Lord will help you to see what this means in your own situation and you will begin to reign with King Jesus.

In Romans 5:17 Paul says, "For if, by the trespass of the one man, death reigned through that one man, how much more will those who receive God's abundant provision of grace and of the gift of righteousness *reign in life through the one man, Jesus Christ*" (emphasis mine). Adam brought us into slavery. Jesus Christ takes us out. We have been made slaves through Adam but in King Jesus we now reign in life. What a marvelous concept!

Sufficiency

You will remember the experience of the apostle Paul. He had a thorn in the flesh. We are not sure what that was; we just know that it was a very discomforting, oppressive and enslaving thing. Paul went to Jesus three times and said, "Lord, take this out of my life." The response was, "No, Paul, I will not remove the thorn. I will give you grace to bear it. My grace will be sufficient for you. My strength will be made perfect in your weakness." (See 2 Corinthians 12:8-9.)

Who is sitting on the throne of grace? It is the Man full of grace, the Lord Jesus. He is prepared to dispense grace to us from above in the measure we need. We need the grace to forgive and to forbear. We need the grace of peace, patience, longsuffering, love, endurance, tenderness, gentleness, strength and power. All of grace in perfection is to be found in the Person of the Lord Jesus. He is the Man full of grace. He sits on the throne of grace to dispense grace to all of us who come.

> Therefore, since we have a great high priest who has gone through the heavens, Jesus the Son of God, let us hold firmly to the faith we profess. For we do not have a high priest who is unable to sympathize with our weaknesses, but we have one who has been tempted in every way, just as we are—yet was without sin. (Hebrews 4:14-15)

Jesus understands us. He lived in this world as a human being. He had human experiences. He knows how to weep. He knew hunger; He experienced pain. He has felt loneliness. He understands all my needs without any exception, and He is up there to minister to all of those needs. That is what the writer to the Hebrews said in 4:16: "Let us then approach the throne of grace with confidence, so that we may receive mercy and find grace to help us in our time of need." We are to come to King Jesus on this throne of grace and petition Him for grace to meet our needs. That grace is always sufficient. That grace always meets our needs. Always.

Security

"For you died, and your life is now hidden with Christ in God" (Colossians 3:3). What a marvelously secure place that is—with Christ in God. You are in the care and keeping of the Father and the Son on the throne of the universe. The devil can't touch you there. The pressures of this world can't touch you there.

I am with Christ. The old life died but my new life is with Christ in God. In a world that is so insecure, we can relax with Christ in the throne room of the universe. Little wonder that Paul says, "Set your minds on things above" (3:2). Sometimes it is said, "Some people are so heavenly-minded that they are no earthly use." That is probably true, but the reverse is just as true—if I am not heavenly-minded I am no earthly use.

In the next segment, Paul abruptly takes us away from this "out of this world experience" and brings us back to planet earth and all the realities that we face here below.

The Believer Has Life Below (3:5-10)

"Put to death, therefore, whatever belongs to your earthly nature" (3:5). Does a heavenly mind know how to deal with earthly problems? Yes. Does a heavenly focus make us practical? Yes. Does having our attention and faith on the Lord Jesus

Christ enable us to deal with life as it is in the nitty gritty? Yes. If we don't start up there we won't succeed down here. That is the whole point. We must be an *above person* if we are to live below with any success or victory. We start where the apostle starts—at the throne of God. You can't start any higher than that. Then you deal with the problems below. The apostle begins teaching our *position* before teaching our *practice*.

Determine what your position is and then you will know what your practice should be. You will have the ability to handle the day-to-day temptations and problems. You will be able to deal with those here below if you have first of all sought the things which are above. We are to do three things as we live out the Christian life.

We are to put to death the members of our bodies.

We have died historically in Christ but now we are to put to death, on a daily basis and on a practical level, all the "members" (NKJV) of our bodies (3:5). What died on the cross in Christ is now to be put to death. The members of our body are not to be instruments of evil. These are to be instruments for God. He is to control the temple, my body. He is to be here living through me.

Notice what we are to put to death: "sexual immorality, impurity, lust, evil desires and greed, which is idolatry. Because of these, the wrath of God is coming" (3:5-6). You used to walk in these ways in the life you once lived. This is your past. It must not control you in the present. Put to death, every day, every member so that these members of the physical body will not be instruments of unrighteousness.

We are to put off sinful practices.

We put to death and then we put off certain sinful practices. "But now you yourselves are to put off all these: anger, wrath, malice, blasphemy, filthy language out of your mouth. Do not lie to one another, since you have put off the old man with his deeds" (3:8-9, NKJV.) Someone has called this portion "The Christian's Dressing Closet."

Get the picture. The imagery is important. We are known often by what we wear, by our clothing. If a man is wearing dirty clothing, you know he has been doing dirty work. Paul said to take off the dirty clothing and fling them away. (It is a strong expression in the Greek.) Get rid of them. Put them in the garbage bin, never to wear them again. Put them off.

We are to put on the new self (man).

It is not enough to put away the filthy garments of the self-life. We must now put on the beautiful garments of the new self. This new self will increasingly experience a deeper knowledge of the Creator and will reflect His image more and more (3:10).

John tells us that the bride of Christ will be clothed in fine linen garments that are white and clean (Revelation 19:8). These garments speak of the righteous acts of the saints. Our character will be seen in our clothing!

Let's begin preparing for that great wedding day now!

The Believer Has Life Within (Colossians 3:11)

"But Christ is all, and is in all" (3:11). Christ is all. That tells us who He is. Christ is all righteousness. He is all wisdom. He is all goodness, all grace, all forgiveness. He is all peace. He is all joy. He is all strength and all power. Christ is all. That is who He is.

This Person who is all has come to live in all of us. What a marvelous thing! It is too big really to believe if it were not in the Bible. This infinitely wonderful Person, this Person who is immeasurable in all of His character and all of His attributes and all of His being, this Person whom the heavens can't contain has come to live in all of us. That is a great truth. Paul said, "There is no Greek or Jew, circumcised or uncircumcised, barbarian, Scythian, slave or free, but Christ is all, and is in all" (3:11).

The poorest believer in this world has as much of Jesus Christ living in him as the richest believer. The weakest saint, the most physically incapable person in the church of God has as much of Jesus Christ living in him as the one who is strong. There are no cultural, racial or social groupings within the household of faith. Jesus shows no favoritism. He came to live in all of His people. That is what brings us together. That is what gives us unity and oneness. We are all believers in Christ, and Christ—all of Him—is in all of us. Dr. Moule says:

> Paul has to meet the "Colossian heresy" and he meets it all along, all around, and all through with Jesus Christ the all satisfying, all sufficient Saviour and Lord. It is just *Himself,* nothing else, nothing less. It is Christ, glorious and personal; not Christ as a mere formula for certain ideas but the divine-human Lord "in all things preeminent," in nature, in grace, in the church, in the soul, for pardon through His cross, for life through His life, for glory through His appearing. To have Him and to make use of Him is peace and power and purity. To do without Him is impossible; it is death. To use Him only partially is perpetual unrest and disappointment. He must be "all things in all things." Then there shall be a great calm within and a great strength and great holiness with it and at last an "appearing with Him in glory" to crown the process and give it its development forever. Even so, Lord Jesus. Be nothing short of "all things in all things," to us in this our Colosse now, where ever it is.[2]

Christ is all and in all.

The Believer Has Life Beyond

Many people do not believe there is a beyond. They live for the here and now. But the beyond is the best. The beyond is when we come into the fullness of all that Jesus Christ is. We are people who live in hope, with the beyond as a beckoning reality. "When Christ, who is your life, appears, then you also will appear with him in glory" (3:4). Three great statements are found here.

Christ is our life.

The Christian life is not an imitated life, a self-driven life, a religious life for the weekend, a life lived in a slightly higher plane or a life of rules and regulations. The Christian life is Christ! He is our life. He doesn't just give me life—He *is* my life. He Himself comes into me, inhabits me, lives in me and gives me Himself. That is a glorious truth. "For to me, *to live is Christ* and to die is gain," Paul said (Philippians 1:21, emphasis mine). The Christian life is the Christ-life.

Christ who is our life will appear.

That word "appear" in the Greek is the idea of coming to full manifestation. The Lord Jesus is coming not just to make an appearance but to manifest Himself. We are going to see Him in all of His glory. He will appear.

Paul said in First Corinthians 13:12, "For now we see in a mirror, dimly, but *then face to face*" (NKJV, emphasis mine). Hebrews 9:28 says, "To those who eagerly wait for Him He will appear a second time" (NKJV). Christ will appear a second time for those who wait eagerly for Him. Are you waiting for Him? Do you live life in this dimension or life *beyond the immediate*?

We will appear with Him in glory.

Christ who is our life will appear, but we also will appear with Him. Notice the prepositional phrase "with him in glory" (Colossians 3:4). In a parallel passage Paul said, "After that, we who are still alive and are left will be caught up together with them in the clouds to meet the Lord in the air. And so *we will be with the Lord* forever. Therefore encourage each other with these words" (1 Thessalonians 4:17-18, emphasis mine).

Yes, with Him! This is the only hope and the ultimate experience of all believers. Be encouraged!

Questions for Reflection or Discussion

1. Discuss how the epistle divides and the significance of this.
2. What are the four dimensions of life that we considered in this chapter?
3. In what way are we to be "heavenly minded"?
4. All believers have shared in a fourfold experience with the Lord Jesus. Explain.
5. Why was there not a chair in the tabernacle or temple?
6. Discuss the three things we believers have in our enthroned Lord.
7. What does Paul's statement "Christ is all, and is in all" mean to you?
8. How does Jesus bring down all cultural and racial barriers?
9. When will the believer have the ultimate spiritual experience? Why?

Endnotes

1. Horatius Bonar, quoted in H.C.G. Moule, *Colossians Studies* (New York: Hodder and Stoughton, 1898), p. 186.
2. Moule, pp. 168-169.

Christit:
Doing All in His Name

Colossians 3:12-17

Therefore, as God's chosen people, holy and dearly loved, clothe yourselves with compassion, kindness, humility, gentleness and patience. Bear with each other and forgive whatever grievances you may have against one another. Forgive as the Lord forgave you. And over all these virtues put on love, which binds them all together in perfect unity.

Let the peace of Christ rule in your hearts, since as members of one body you were called to peace. And be thankful. Let the word of Christ dwell in you richly as you teach and admonish one another with all wisdom, and as you sing psalms, hymns and spiritual songs with gratitude in your hearts to God. And whatever you do, whether in word or deed, do it all in the name of the Lord Jesus, giving thanks to God the Father through him.

What a tremendous passage this is! It is interesting to observe that Paul identified believers in three ways in 3:12.

1. He called us "God's chosen people." We were chosen in Christ before the foundation of the world, which tells us that election is by sovereign grace alone, not by human merit. We are the elect of God.

2. He said we are "holy." That is, we are the people whom God has set apart to be His special people. In the Old Testament the holy people were the Israelis, the sons and daughters of Abraham. They were chosen to be a holy nation. They were a nation set apart from all the nations of the world to be a special people for God and to express and demonstrate and teach His holiness. They received the holy Scriptures. They had a holy priesthood. They had a holy tabernacle and a holy temple and they were to live holy lives. This was all to be in contrast to the pagan environment around them.

3. We are called "dearly loved" ones. God loves us with an everlasting love—enough to give His Son to die in our place. He will never fall out of love with us. We can hurt His heart, walk away from Him or do many things which displease Him but He will never cease to love us.

Based on who we are, we are told what to do. Always start with *who you are* as a Christian; then you will discover what you are to do as a Christian. Don't think that you will become what you should be by doing certain things. You will do certain things because the Lord has made you a special person. We are the chosen. We are the holy ones. We are the dearly loved ones. Because of this we will demonstrate certain behavior. We will establish certain values. We will have a certain perspective. Our lives will take on a supernatural quality because of the kind of people we are—the kind of people the Lord, by His grace and power, has made us.

We Are People Who Experience a Godly "Put On" (3:12-14)

Paul said we should, as people of God, "put on tender mercies" (3:12, NKJV). You will remember in the last chapter we saw that we are to put off certain things like a dirty, filthy garment and never take them back again. If the people of God are to be holy in their lives, they must put off certain things: "You must rid yourselves of all such things as these: anger, rage, malice, slander, and filthy language from your lips. Do not lie to each other" (3:8-9). The next step is to put on certain character qualities, certain virtues. There are eight of them here and each one of them is a sermon in itself.

Put on tender mercies, or compassion (3:12).

This means to put on compassion, to see and feel people's needs and then move by what we see and feel to meet the needs. Compassion sees the need and doesn't just say, "Isn't that too bad," but goes, binds up the wounds and ministers to the person. Jesus was moved with compassion when He saw people as sheep without a shepherd. Because of this, He instructed His disciples to pray that the Lord would send workers to help those in need (Matthew 9:36-38).

Put on kindness (Colossians 3:12).

That is, put on goodness of heart that acts generously toward others.

Put on humility (3:12).

Put on lowliness. This is the posture of a slave. Humility was not a character quality that the Romans admired; in fact, they considered it a weakness. But when Jesus came, He demonstrated in His own life that humility is a marvelous character quality. He came not to be served but to serve and to give His life for others. He washed the disciples' feet and then told them that He had given them an example to serve people. We are to have the humility of Christ.

We are to put on meekness, or gentleness (3:12).

Meekness does God's will without murmuring. A meek person is a person who is always in a learning mode, a submissive mode (James 1:21). A meek person says, "I don't know much. I want to know more. I want to be better. I want to learn. Whatever God says, I'll respond to in obedience."

Put on longsuffering, or patience (Colossians 3:12).

This means to exercise patience and self-restraint under provocation. When I am provoked, the natural thing to do is to fly off the handle, to react harshly. Patience helps me stay under control. Barclay says, "Human patience is a reflection of the divine patience, which bears with all our sinning and never casts us off."[1]

Put on forbearance, or bear with each other (3:13).

This means that I do not react in an injurious manner when I am hurt. In other words, when I am hurt I don't hurt back. I forbear. I don't say, "I am going to get even." I don't react negatively.

Put on forgiveness (3:13).

That means to blank out all offenses against me and keep no account of wrongdoing. Sometimes people say, "I'll forgive, but I won't forget." That means they hold a grudge in their heart. It means that they have kept a mental record and have not really forgiven. To forgive means to wipe the slate clean. Suppose Jesus said, "I will forgive you but I will never forget your evil deeds." Would that be forgiveness? Would you find any comfort if you knew that Jesus was keeping an account of all of the evil you had ever done? No, forgiveness goes far deeper than that. We are to forgive even as Jesus forgave.

Put on love (3:14).

"And over all these virtues put on love, which binds them all together in perfect unity" (3:14). That means that we are to put on love over all of these other Christian qualities. In other words, love is to be the outer garment of our spiritual dress. We have seven undergarments, and now there is an outer garment. We don't understand this in the modern Western world because we don't dress like this now. But in the day of Jesus, you had undergarments and outer garments. The outer garment was always fastened with a girdle or a belt or a sash. The outer garment held all of the other garments together. The outer garment was what you saw and it was what was always the most beautiful.

Love is to be the outer garment. It is to bind all the other virtues together. Love is to be the crowning virtue. Can I forgive you if I don't love you? No. Can I be meek if I am not a person of love? No. Can I forbear if I don't have love? No. Am I going to be longsuffering and patient and kind if I don't have love? No. All of these things are stimulated by, motivated by and supported by love. You will remember that in First Corinthians 13:1-3 Paul said that we can do all kinds of good things but if we don't have love we're nothing. Nothing is zero with the rim removed—that is what I am without love. It is the essential character quality, the essential virtue of the Christian life. All of these other things fall right into place if I love you.

We Are People Who Enjoy a Gentle Peace (Colossians 3:15)

The chosen of God are people who not only experience a godly "put on" but they are people who enjoy a gentle peace.

"Let the peace of Christ rule in your hearts, since as members of one body you were called to peace. And be thankful" (3:15). Literally this says, "Let the peace of Christ umpire in your hearts." That is an interesting expression that means that His peace is to be the arbiter whenever conflict or stress enters the fellowship of believers. Enjoying peace is the blessing to which we've been called in the one body of Christ. The peaceful, harmonious function of the one body, in its many parts, is the way that the Lord has designed us to work. I am to *have* peace and I am to *make* peace within the fellowship of God's church. If there is anything that's contrary to the nature of God, it is conflict and division and strife. God is one God. We have been called into one Body, by one Spirit. We love one Lord and we are to be one people in our functions and in our relationships.

This peace is a unique peace. It doesn't come by just gritting your teeth and saying, "I am going to get along with this person if it kills me." That isn't peace—that kind of thinking will cause you to go to pieces!

On the night of His betrayal the Lord Jesus said to His disciples, "Peace I leave with you; my peace I give to you. I do not give to you as the world gives. Do not let your hearts be troubled and do not be afraid" (John 14:27). These disciples were facing anything but peaceful circumstances. They were going to be hated. They were going to be rejected. All of them, perhaps with one exception, would be martyred. They were going to walk right into the jaws of death itself once Jesus went back to heaven.

But Jesus left them with the great legacy of His peace. They would have His peace in their hearts. We live in a troubled world, but that trouble doesn't have to get inside me. It *must not* get inside me. I must have in my heart the peace of Christ.

Paul said, "And be thankful" (Colossians 3:15). "Thankful" is an important word for us always to take to heart. Ungrateful people are always problem people. They are selfish and negative. Recently, after some careful study, the United Nations declared that Canada is the number one place in the world to live. In commenting on this, someone observed that we Canadians lead the world in another category as well. We lead the world in grumbling! Ironic, isn't it?

There should be no "grumblers" in the church. Ours should be the attitude of gratitude!

We Are People Who Express a Gracious Praise (3:16)

Positive, God-honoring praise should rise from the altars of our hearts as the incense in the Old Testament tabernacle arose night and day to God. Our hearts should be an altar from which praise ascends to Him, the aroma of worship. There is a great text for that here: "Let the word of Christ dwell in you richly as you teach and admonish one another with all wisdom, and as you sing psalms, hymns and spiritual songs with gratitude [grace] in your hearts to God" (3:16). Let me give you five things about worship that we have in this text.

The scriptural factor

"Let the word of Christ dwell in you richly." Literally, "Let the Word of Christ be *at home* in your heart richly." God's Word is indeed a rich word. When it finds a home in our hearts we will be greatly enriched. We will never worship God acceptably apart from His Word; He must speak to me before I speak to Him. I must hear from Him before He hears from me. In the Word we learn who He is. There we get the great concepts, the great doctrines, the great principles and the great truths of our great God. As we see Him in the Scriptures we begin to worship Him. Jesus said we must worship in spirit and in truth. The truth will make us worshipers. Revelation before adoration!

The instructional factor

We are to "teach and admonish one another." People are always taught and edified and admonished when we express God's Word in our worship. To teach is to give practical, positive instruction. To admonish is to warn. The Bible does both. It gives us instruction about how to live and it gives us warning about how not to live. The Christian life is to be viewed both as positive and negative, and the Bible will give us both positive and negative truth.

The musical factor

Music—isn't it a wonderful gift? Someone asked me, "If your house was burning down and you had three things to save, what would you save?" My answer was my wife, my Bible and my stereo. I love music. I love Haydn. I love Mozart. I love Bach. I love Beethoven. They have so enriched my life. Augustine, the great church father, says, "There are three essentials of a hymn. It must be praise. It must be addressed to God. And it must be sung." God help us to be always a singing Church.

The internal factor

"Singing with grace *in your hearts*" (3:16, NKJV, emphasis added). Only hearts touched by the grace of God can really express proper praise. "Sing and make music in your heart" is what Paul said in Ephesians 5:19. Oh God, give us singing hearts. Your heart may sing but what comes out may be awful. That's all right. God listens to the heart. That is where He hears the song. You may sound like a bullfrog with laryngitis, but it doesn't matter! Sing in your heart and from your heart.

The vertical factor

We are to do all of this "to God" (Colossians 3:16). Sing to God. Worship God. It is praise, not performance!

We Are People Who Embrace a Great .

"Whatever you do, whether in word or deec
name of the Lord Jesus, giving thanks to Gc
through him" (3:17). This great text sets forth a pi.
has a very broad application to us as believers. It provi.   .d-
ance for us in every situation we will ever encounter. Th.ɔ principle means at least three things.

Jesus is represented when I speak and do things in His name.

When I bear the name of the Lord Jesus Christ, I represent
Him in the world. Paul speaks in another place about us being
His ambassadors (2 Corinthians 5:20). We are the official rep-
resentatives of the King of heaven!

Long before I knew the Lord Jesus, I knew His representatives. They were in my family and they lived in my community.
I learned much about the Christian life by watching their conduct and listening to their prayers. I learned that the Word of
God is precious, that prayer is vital, that personal purity and in-
tegrity are essential. I learned that gathering with the Lord's
people on the Lord's Day took priority over other activities. I
learned that Jesus alone can save from sin.

I learned all of these things before I became a Christian from
good representatives of our Lord who practiced the principle of
Colossians 3:17.

I am authorized.

When I act, speak or pray in Jesus' name, I say that He has
authorized me or empowered me to do so. Please recall the
words of Peter to the lame man at the gate called Beautiful, "In
the name of Jesus Christ of Nazareth, walk" (Acts 3:6). Peter
didn't say, "In my name, walk" or "In the name of the church,
walk" or "In the name of the apostles, walk." He was saying, "I
have been authorized to say this to you by King Jesus. I am au-

..orized and empowered to say this to you, my crippled friend: in Jesus' name, rise up and walk."

When we speak to people in Jesus' name we are saying, "I am authorized, I am called, I am empowered to minister Christ to you."

The Father is thanked when my words and ways are expressed in Jesus' name.

When I act in Jesus' name, it is in order that God the Father be thanked through Him. If what I say will not bring thanksgiving to God then I must not say it. If what I do will not bring thanksgiving to God then I must not do it. Whatever I say, whatever I do, is to be to His glory. It is a great test. Jesus said, "I will do whatever you ask in *my name,* so that *the Son may bring glory to the Father*" (John 14:13, emphasis mine). In another place, Paul said, "Therefore, whether you eat or drink, or whatever you do, do all *to the glory of God*" (1 Corinthians 10:31, NKJV, emphasis mine).

Colossians 3:17 is really a summary of the verses that have preceded it. But ultimately it underscores again the great theme of this epistle—the supremacy of Christ. Christ is to be supreme and sovereign in all of life.

Questions for Reflection or Discussion

1. How are we as believers identified in 3:12?
2. Discuss the spiritual virtues that we are to be clothed with. What are we to "put on"?
3. In what person are these virtues perfectly demonstrated?
4. Discuss the factors involved in praising the Lord in our gatherings.
5. What does it mean to do all things in the name of the Lord Jesus?

Endnote

1. William Barclay, *The Letters to the Philippians, Colossians, and Thessalonians,* Daily Bible Studies (Toronto, ON: Welch Co., 1956), p. 158.

10

Christ: In Our Homes

Colossians 3:18-4:1

Wives, submit to your husbands, as is fitting in the Lord.
Husbands, love your wives and do not be harsh with them.
Children, obey your parents in everything, for this pleases the Lord.
Fathers, do not embitter your children, or they will become discouraged.
Slaves, obey your earthly masters in everything; and do it, not only when their eye is on you and to win their favor, but with sincerity of heart and reverence for the Lord. Whatever you do, work at it with all your heart, as working for the Lord, not for men, since you know that you will receive an inheritance from the Lord as a reward. It is the Lord Christ you are serving. Anyone who does wrong will be repaid for his wrong, and there is no favoritism.
Masters, provide your slaves with what is right and fair, because you know that you also have a Master in heaven.

In this chapter we go from the heavenlies to the home . . . from the dwelling place of our Lord to the dwelling place of our families . . . from the sublime to the common. I think it is instructive to observe that the climax of the profound truths Paul has been developing does not find its primary application in some great project or spiritual endeavor, but rather in the home. If we have truly "set [our] hearts on things above" (see 3:2), it will be clearly seen in how we take our responsibilities and respect one another here below.

Paul gave us here in our text some very simple and straightforward rules and principles that apply to family relationships. These are not to be looked at, however, without understanding that all of them will work only as we recognize the presence and preeminence of Christ in our Christian homes. Look at the repeated reference to our Lord: "in the Lord" (3:18); "this pleases the Lord" (3:20); "reverence for the Lord" (3:22); "working for the Lord" (3:23); "inheritance from the Lord" (3:24); "you also have a Master in heaven" (4:1).

I remember reading somewhere that C.S. Lewis believed that if the home is a means of grace, it must also be a place of rules. Without rules, the family will live under the tyranny of the most selfish member. Someone else has said, "As in improvised music, spontaneity and freedom do not mean playing out of tune." We are to be in tune in the home. We are to be in sync.

I have a role to fill; my wife has a role to fill; my children have other roles to fill. I can't fill my wife's role; she can't fill my role; we can't fill the children's roles. Each of us has a tune to play, but we must be on key, and we must play together in harmony. When we do, then we have a home that makes beautiful music. The rules are so simple and yet we find them difficult to embrace at times. We have a tendency to read in things or take things out or adjust them to the thinking of modern culture. It is difficult for us to take the words off the page and say, "These words are for me here and now in my home today, and they will work because they are words from the Lord Himself."

You will notice in the passage that we have three vital domestic relationships set forward for believers. The first is the relationship between husband and wife, the second between parents and children and the third between masters and slaves. Someone might question how instruction concerning masters and slaves has any relevance today. It is quite true that we don't have a slave culture today, but principles that applied to masters and slaves of Paul's day certainly apply to employer and employee relationships now.

The reason why Paul put it here is because in his day this was a part of the domestic scene. In most households there were masters and slaves. The slaves were there to do the will of the master, to make his life comfortable and to be productive members of his household. There were 60 million slaves during this period in history. There were more slaves in the Roman Empire then than there had been in all preceding history. Paul will show that even slavery, at the very bottom of the social scale, can be a place of joy, productivity and spiritual fulfillment. There is no place in life where I cannot serve Jesus if I will trust Him to give me the grace to do it. The first important relationship in the home is the relationship between . . .

Husband and Wife (3:18-19)

The wives, according to the text, are to submit to their husband's leadership and headship in the home (3:18). This is not slavish subordination but the simple recognition that the husband has been divinely appointed to lead the family. Submission is viewed today in some circles, and particularly by radical feminists, as a very negative word, a word that has no place in modern society. After all, don't we have equal rights? We are not here looking at rights as much as at responsibilities. Paul was talking about filling the roles that have been divinely given to us in the home.

Husbands are to love their wives, as we soon will learn, and the wife submits to that loving leadership. I think that it is important to understand that Paul here was not speaking about the husband being superior to the wife. It has nothing to do with his value or his worth or her value or her worth. Both are equal in value. Both are equal in worth. Paul states this in Galatians 3:28: "There is neither Jew nor Greek, slave nor free, male nor female, for you are all one in Christ Jesus."

Our spiritual equality, however, does not mean that we are equal in the *roles* that we are to assume in the home. Our roles as husbands and wives are distinctive.

Permitting the husband to lead does not in any way cancel the wife's giftedness or unique contribution in the home and the church. She is as much a member of the body of Christ as is the husband. Indeed, there are many times when the husband must seek the wisdom and insights of his wife where he is making decisions. He will often "submit" to her spiritual counsel, but the primary leadership responsibility remains his, and for this he is held accountable by the Lord.

The husbands are instructed in our text to love their wives. In Ephesians 5:25, Paul enlarges on this and says that we men are to love our wives just as Christ loved the Church and gave Himself for her. This means that my wife must come first. Love—Christ's love—is self-giving love. It is self-sacrificing love. When I have His love I will look after the concerns and needs of my wife.

When we men take the responsibility of headship in our homes, it is vital that we take it from Him who is the Head of the Church and realize that He gave His life for the Church. He died for His bride!

So I say to all of us who are husbands—we are to be the personification and the demonstration of love in our homes. Whatever love does, that is what we are supposed to do. Whatever love is, that is what we are supposed to be. God help us to be lovers. Let us set a pattern for our sons so that someday, if they are married, they will remember the love they saw in us and repeat it in their relationship with their wives.

The second important relationship in the home is the relationship between . . .

Parents and Children (Colossians 3:20-21)

The implication of 3:20 is that the parents are instructing, directing and disciplining their children. Obeying someone presupposes that that person has given you something to obey. Parents cannot be silent. Parents must be teachers. Parents must discipline. Parents must set guidelines. Parents must establish standards. Parents are to be the people who set the spiritual pace for the children in the home. Children are to respond in obedience. There are few verses in the Bible that are addressed to children but here is one of them. It is so simple. You don't have to be a theologian to understand. It says, "Obey your parents." Children, give them honor. Do what they tell you to do. If you do not learn the blessing of obedience in the home it will be extremely difficult for you to practice obedience anywhere else in society. It will be hard for you to obey the teacher or the principal or the boss or the military commander or the police officer or anyone else who has the responsibility of seeing that rules are carried out and regulations are maintained! We have an orderly society when people obey, but when people stop obeying, then we have anarchy and our society is destroyed. We begin to build a strong society in the home.

Our text says that children are to obey their parents in everything "for this pleases the Lord." The primary purpose for every life, of course, is to please the Lord. The ultimate in parents instructing their children and the children carrying out those instructions is to please the Lord. The Lord is never pleased with failure on either end.

In our very indulgent culture some parents care more about pleasing their children than in pleasing the Lord. They put their children at the center of the family and try to cater to their immature desires in a vain attempt to make them happy. This is a sure formula for raising spoiled children and creating major conflicts in the home.

Parents must be consistent in their requirements of their children and must be fair in what they ask them to do. We must treat them with respect and we must always be an example of what we teach them to do. Children dislike rule-breakers and hypocrites. They have a kind of built-in sense of right and wrong. How many times have we heard them say, "That isn't fair!"? We parents must honor that God-given conscience and seek to be as even-handed and fair with them as possible.

Obviously we understand that what we ask them to do will be the Christian thing. We will be guided by the Word of God and by the Holy Spirit in the sorts of things we instruct our children to do. We must have this in place before we insist on their obedience.

Let me give you some proverbs that are helpful.

- My son, do not forget my law, but let your heart keep my commands; for length of days and long life and peace they will add to you. Let not mercy and truth forsake you; bind them around your neck, write them on the tablet of your heart, and so find favor and high esteem in the sight of God and man. (Proverbs 3:1-4, NKJV)

- My son, give attention to my words; incline your ear to my sayings. Do not let them depart from your eyes; keep them in the midst of your heart; for they are life to those who find them, and health to all their flesh. (4:20-22, NKJV)

- My son, keep your father's command, and do not forsake the law of your mother. Bind them continually upon your heart; tie them around your neck. When you roam, they will lead you; when you sleep, they will keep you; and when you awake, they will speak with you. (6:20-22, NKJV)

This shows that both father and mother are teachers of the children. It shows that the father supports what the mother says and she supports what the father says. The parents are saying the same thing to the children. Each parent honors the other parent. This is a team effort of teaching and the child must understand that.

Fathers are given an additional word in our Colossians text at 3:21. "Fathers, do not embitter your children, or they will become discouraged." In a parallel passage in Ephesians, Paul says, "Do not exasperate your children" (6:4). In other words, don't demand unreasonable things that will cause a strong reaction from your children. As a father, I should be the means of solving problems, not causing them. I shouldn't be an irritant to my children. I should be a supporter and a lover and an approver and an affirmer.

Of course there are times of discipline. Of course there are times when the child won't like what I say or do as a parent. That is understandable because they are immature. They don't understand why these things are necessary. Someday they will, but meanwhile we must insist that they honor us and follow our instructions.

But I must not, with severe punishment, with nagging or with a kind of heavy-handedness, cause my child to react and become angry with me. I think sometimes children find it difficult to come to church and listen to anything the pastor or teacher says because they are so offended by their parents. They have problems with all authority figures because they are upset with those of us who represent authority in the home.

In concluding this section, I would like to say a word about the importance of us parents helping our children understand that the instruction in Colossians 3:20 is addressed specifically to them. This is the Word of God to them. They must deal directly with the Lord Himself regarding the matter of obedience.

In other words, this is not a *horizontal issue between parent and child* as much as it is a *vertical issue between God and child.* What I as a parent say to the child doesn't matter nearly as much as what God says to the child. The child can understand this.

Once, when one of our children had disobeyed me, I had the child sit with me and read aloud the words of Paul in Ephesians 6:1-2, "Children, obey your parents in the Lord, for this is right. 'Honor your father and mother'—which is the first commandment with promise—'that it may go well with you and that you may enjoy long life on the earth.' " I vividly recall the tremor in the voice and the flowing tears as God spoke directly to my child. That was a defining moment—a divine encounter that changed that young life forever.

The third important relationship our text speaks about is the relationship between . . .

Masters and Servants (Colossians 3:22-4:1)

What slaves were to do

They were to obey their masters in all things. This fits in our culture in the employee-employer relationship. If Paul were writing to us today, he would say, "Employees, obey your employer in everything." As a Christian employee, the best person in your company should be you. The person who works the hardest for your company should be you. The person who says all the good things he or she can say about a company should be you.

How slaves were to do it

They were not to give with "eye service." That is, they were not to serve just when the boss was looking. Do we do that in our companies, in our businesses? When the boss is away, when the manager is out of the office, when the supervisor is off the floor, are we still as vigorous and intense and committed and loyal and faithful as when they are watching us?

The slave was also to serve "with sincerity of heart." He was to render his work with a real heart for what he was doing. I'm sure we have all worked with people who had "no heart" for the job. What they did was carried out in a perfunctory manner and with little enthusiasm. It is not a pleasant experience.

The Christian slave was to do all that he did with "reverence for the Lord." The Bible makes no distinction between sacred and secular. All of life, including the lowliest of tasks, is to be carried out in a reverential manner. We must practice His presence everywhere and at all times. What a difference this makes on the job!

"Whatever you do, work at it with all your heart, as working for the Lord, not for men" (3:23). Many in the workplace never see this principle, and work becomes a drudgery and a pointless effort. The people who feel this way think that the only work for God is done at church and most particularly by people called to do His work. No! All work is God's work and should be carried out for Him. What a wonderfully elevating effect this has upon us when we are doing jobs that may be boring and not in the least fulfilling.

Why slaves were to do it

Slaves were to serve knowing that the ultimate in their service was to receive an inheritance from the Lord Jesus as their reward (3:24).

This must have been an enormously encouraging word to the slaves in Colosse. Dr. Barclay has this comment,

> Here was an amazing thing. Under Roman law a slave could not possess any property whatsoever and here

he is being promised nothing less than the inheritance
of God. He must remember that the time will come
when the balance is adjusted and evil doing will find
its punishment and faithful diligence its reward.[1]

In like manner, the modern workman must serve the Lord
through his company and know that great reward is not the salary and benefits but the rich and eternal reward of his Lord. If
indeed these truths are real in the life of modern employees, we
will be able to stop saying, "Thank God it's Friday" and begin
to say, "Thank God it's Monday."

Paul now turns his attention to the masters of the slaves.
"Masters, provide your slaves with what is right and fair, because you know that you also have a Master in heaven" (4:1).
There is only one absolute Master and He is the Lord in heaven.
What a difference it makes when all authority figures remember this.

The primary purpose of any boss is to provide for his employees, not take from them. He is to provide fair wages and
good working conditions. He is to treat them the way Jesus
treats His servants. What radical changes would take place in
the workplace if these instructions were carried out today!

Conclusion

We are not all the same in the structure and function of the
Christian home. Even though we are all equal in value and
worth, we each have a distinctive role with distinctive responsibilities that each of those roles brings.

In all of society, there are leaders and followers, people who
are over, people who are under, people with authority, people
who are subordinate to authority—and the home is where all of
this is first practiced and demonstrated. This is where these
principles are seen in their purest and simplest form. This is
how we learn to be respectable, accountable and productive cit-

izens in our society. We learn it in the home. That is where we learn obedience. That is where we learn to love. That is where we learn to submit. That is where we learn to care for a particular role that has been given to us. That is where we learn to respect people.

We learn not only from what Paul has said concerning the home but we learn as well from *what he does not say*. He says nothing about a live-in boyfriend-girlfriend relationship, nothing about a so-called "common law" arrangement. To him, marriage is governed by sacred law, not by common law. He also does not say anything about same-sex marriages. If same-sex marriages were legitimate and to be a part of the Christian community there certainly would have been instructions from the inspired writers of Scriptures about them.

Paul has been defining what a truly Christian home is and therefore the Lord Himself is totally involved. Review again these terms: "in the Lord" (3:18), "to the Lord" (3:20, NKJV), "fearing God" (3:22, NKJV), "for the Lord" (3:23), "from the Lord" (3:24), "serve the Lord Christ" (3:24, NKJV) and "Master in heaven" (4:1). All say most strongly that we do not have a Christian home by just trying to follow a few rules and practice a little religion. A Christian home has Christ as its source, as its center, as its life, as its peace, as its instructor, as its Savior. A true Christian home has Christ in its very heart. The home revolves around Him. The home comes from Him. The home must praise Him. There is no Christian home without Christ.

Finally, all that Paul said before this text concerning the supremacy and preeminence of Christ has given us a most profound Christology, and because of that, a most profound Christian life. It may seem, therefore, almost anticlimactic for us now to look at what appears to be rather mundane instruction about things that on the surface look rather ordinary. But to think this way is to miss the fact that in the New Testament epistles, great doctrine is always followed by simple application to life wherever life is lived.

There is no place where the great truths concerning Christ should be more practically apparent than in the home. This is where we really live. This is where we must experience Christ and live Christ and show Christ as in no other place or relationship. My Christian life will be seen to be what it really and truly is in the way I conduct myself in the home. If you want to find out what kind of person I am, don't ask the Board of Elders, don't ask my staff, don't ask my District Superintendent, don't even ask my congregation. Ask my wife, ask my children and grandchildren. They know me off the platform. They know me when I'm not called reverend or pastor. They know me when I am not held up in some kind of artificial elevation as the leader. They know me at the kitchen table. They know me in the day-to-day interactions of life. They know me in my home where I really live out the kind of person I am.

We can and must practice the presence and principles of Christ in our homes. The home is under increasing attack and the only sure defense is not more counseling or more books or more seminars *but more of Him!*

Questions for Reflection or Discussion

1. How does this third chapter of Colossians "go from the heavenlies to the home"?

2. Discuss the roles that the husband and wife are to fill in the home. How do they differ and how do they complement each other?

3. Why is it essential that children learn to respect and obey their parents?

4. How can we help children understand that God says some things directly to them?

5. How do we "exasperate" our children? How can we stop?

6. What is the ultimate reason for obeying parents?

7. How can instruction to masters and slaves have any meaning to us today?

8. What makes doing ordinary work assignments very meaningful to the believer?

Endnote

1. William Barclay, *The Letters to the Philippians, Colossians, and Thessalonians,* Daily Bible Studies (Toronto, ON: Welch Co., 1956), p. 165.

11

Christ: Serving Him

Colossians 4:2-18

Devote yourselves to prayer, being watchful and thankful. And pray for us, too, that God may open a door for our message, so that we may proclaim the mystery of Christ, for which I am in chains. Pray that I may proclaim it clearly, as I should. Be wise in the way you act toward outsiders; make the most of every opportunity. Let your conversation be always full of grace, seasoned with salt, so that you may know how to answer everyone.

Tychicus will tell you all the news about me. He is a dear brother, a faithful minister and fellow servant in the Lord. I am sending him to you for the express purpose that you may know about our circumstances and that he may encourage your hearts. He is coming with Onesimus, our faithful and dear brother, who is one of you. They will tell you everything that is happening here.

My fellow prisoner Aristarchus sends you his greetings, as does Mark, the cousin of Barnabas. (You have received instructions about him; if he comes to you, welcome him.) Jesus, who is called Justus, also sends greetings. These are the only Jews among my fellow workers for the kingdom of God, and they have proved a comfort to me. Epaphras, who is one of you and a servant of Christ Jesus, sends greetings. He is always wrestling in prayer for you, that you may stand firm in all the will of God, mature and fully assured. I vouch for him that he is working hard for you and for those

135

*at Laodicea and Hierapolis. Our dear friend Luke, the doctor, and
Demas send greetings. Give my greetings to the brothers at
Laodicea, and to Nympha and the church in her house.*

*After this letter has been read to you, see that it is also read in the
church of the Laodiceans and that you in turn read the letter from
Laodicea.*

*Tell Archippus: "See to it that you complete the work you have
received in the Lord."*

*I, Paul, write this greeting in my own hand. Remember my
chains. Grace be with you.*

In the portion before us we can learn some important lessons
about service for our Lord. The teacher, of course, is the
apostle Paul. He was writing from a Roman prison cell with a
chain on his wrist. This tells us at the very outset that our service may occur in the most unlikely places. Ministering for the
Savior doesn't require an ideal situation.

Our message divides into two headings. In the first we are
looking at the believer's service to outsiders. In the second
heading we are looking at the believer's service to the insiders!

The Believer's Service to Outsiders (4:2-6)

There are only two groups of people today in the world. They
are not rich and poor, high and low, good and bad. They are not
Westerners and Easterners. They are the outsiders and the insiders—those in Christ, and those not in Christ. Those who are
outside are outside of Christ's Church, outside of the fellowship of His saints. They are outside of the ministry that God has
committed to His people in this world. Paul used the expression
"outsiders" in 4:5.

How do we bridge the gap to outsiders? How do we get to the
people who are outside the walls of this church? I believe that
many outsiders would like to be insiders. They don't like it out
there. It is a cold, hostile, selfish, dark world on its way to de-

struction. There are tremendous feelings of insecurity today among the outsiders.

Some of you who read these words were outsiders just a short while ago. But you are insiders now. You are in Christ, in fellowship with His people. You are the happiest you have ever been. Life has taken on a meaning that you never knew as an outsider. May your tribe increase in the land! May more outsiders become insiders.

So let's go to the outsiders. Let's learn how to build bridges to them. Let's learn how to love them. Let's learn how to reach out to them in the name of Christ and bring them in.

Pray.

First of all, and above all, we pray. That's what Paul encouraged the Colossians to do. In 4:2, he said, "Devote yourselves to prayer." We are to be faithful in prayer. We are not to give up in our praying. We are to pray with watchfulness. That word in the Greek means to be wakeful. We are to be awake when we pray. Perhaps Paul was thinking of the time when the disciples went to sleep in the Garden of Gethsemane. They should have been watching and praying with Jesus in that critical hour, but they went to sleep. Oh, may God arouse us today out of our slumber, out of our spiritual sleep, and give us an alertness in our praying.

They were to pray with thanksgiving. Go through this little epistle and underline the times you find thanksgiving referred to. You will find it often. Paul's life was a thankful life, and his epistles were filled with thanksgiving. He encouraged the people of God everywhere he went to be thankful people.

Then they were to pray for those who were directly involved in preaching and teaching the gospel. "And pray for us, too" (4:3). Paul wasn't a super-saint. He was mortal, with weaknesses and needs. He asked the church in Colosse to pray for them. "Pray for us here in prison, those of us who are prisoners

of Jesus Christ," he asked. "Pray that God would open us a door
for the Word." Notice he didn't say, "Pray that the prison door
will open," although I am sure he would have been very pleased
to have had that happen. In fact, in other writings he does ask
people to pray for his release. But he is concerned here about an
open door for the Word of God.

God can open a door while you are locked up. God can open
a door when you can't do anything. God can open a door of
ministry to you when you don't feel that you have any ability or
any opportunity. God has wonderful ways of opening doors
even when all the material, physical, natural doors are closed.

And do you know what happened? God did open a door.
There was a Roman soldier sitting at the end of the chain that
was around the apostle's wrist. That soldier heard the gospel,
you can be sure of that. And they changed the guard regularly.
So Paul got a different audience every few hours. How would
you like to be locked up with Paul in prison? Don't you think
you would hear the Word of God?

These guards were a part of the praetorium. This was a group
of about 9,000 imperial guards. They were the choicest of all
the Roman soldiers and were committed to the security of
Caesar and his palace.

The result of these providential encounters was that some of
these men were converted, the gospel was "advanced"
(Philippians 1:12) and many came to Christ in Caesar's household (4:22). Little wonder then that Paul was requesting prayer
that doors would continue to open for his message. You may
lock up God's servant but you cannot lock up His Word or His
Spirit. God has His own way of making "openings."

God will open doors. He can open doors to outsiders in your
business or in your home or in your school. He can open doors
to outsiders wherever you are. If you and I are alert and prayer-
ful, He will open doors so that the Word of God can be given to

people. He will give us creative ways of doing it. He will show us things to do that perhaps we have never done before.

Make the most of every opportunity.

A second factor in our ministry to outsiders is that we are to be "wise in the way [we] act toward outsiders; make the most of every opportunity" (Colossians 4:5). We should be wise in the way we give the gospel. We should be winsome. We should be careful. We should think before we speak. Our message should suit the person to whom we are giving it. We can think of all kinds of ways of building bridges of love, walking in wisdom toward those who are on the outside.

Be careful how you talk.

A third factor in reaching "outsiders" is expressed in 4:6: "Let your conversation be always full of grace, seasoned with salt, so that you may know how to answer everyone." Not *what* to answer—all of us know what to answer. We are all theologians ready to quote verses. But do we know *how* to say it, and when to say it? You don't get that from soul-winner's classes. You don't get that out of books. You get that from the Holy Spirit, who alone will make you wise to witness. He will help you know what to say, how to say it and when to say it. We need to be "graced" speakers. We need much grace when we speak to outsiders. Many of you reading this are believers because someone spoke graciously to you.

"So all bore witness to Him, and marveled at the gracious words which proceeded out of His mouth" (Luke 4:22, NKJV). Who is this Person with gracious words, this Person who speaks graciously? It is the Lord Jesus, of course. People marveled at His gracious words because they were hearing hard, harsh, legalistic words from the Pharisees: keep the law, keep the ceremonies, keep the rituals, keep the traditions. They were weary of all of that.

Then Jesus came, the carpenter's son, and spoke gracious words, because He is the man full of grace and truth. Jesus speaks the grace of forgiveness, the grace of eternal life, the grace of joy and the grace of blessing. Every time we speak to people on the outside we should speak as the oracle of God. We should speak with the gracious words of our gracious Lord. If we are filled with the Spirit of Christ He will help us to be gracious people.

God help us to be not just theologically sound but "speaking the truth in love" as Paul expressed it in Ephesians 4:15.

We come now to the second division of our text.

The Believer's Service to Insiders (Colossians 4:7-18)

In this section of the passage we have several people named who are serving on the "inside," that is, serving the church. Paul gives us a wonderful list of servants of Christ who have made sacred history. Let me tell you this: if you will serve the Lord Jesus with wisdom and with grace you will make sacred history also—not political history, business history, social history or educational history, as important as they might be. You will make history that is really His story!

We know about these people because 2,000 years ago they served the Lord Jesus Christ and God took note of that and put their names in the Bible. We would have never known them if they hadn't served Jesus. They would have been just more statistics in the Roman census. But they served Jesus Christ and because they served Him we know about them. The shadow of their lives falls across your life and mine today and we are better people because of Tychicus and Onesimus and Aristarchus and Mark and Justus and Epaphras and Luke and Demas. Dr. Charles Erdman says this about them:

> The names of the friends grouped around that of the apostle form a brilliant galaxy shining like stars

around a central sun. The mere mention of these names in the various epistles of Paul adds to his writings a tone of reality and an element of deep human interest. The letters are made to be not mere theological essays, or moral homilies, but vital messages to living men illustrated and embodied in actual life. In no portion of his letters, excepting possibly the last chapter of the epistle to the Romans, does Paul give a more fascinating list of his companions than in the closing or personal section of this epistle to the Colossians. This paragraph may be viewed as a portrait gallery of Paul's friends, or as constituting an entertaining volume of missionary biography.[1]

The theme here is service. The language is that of service. Let me give you some of the language: "faithful minister," "fellow servant" (4:7), "fellow workers" (4:11), "servant of Christ Jesus" (4:12), "working hard" (4:13). The theme is service. The service rendered by Paul and his friends to each other and the church can be defined in five words.

Unity

These people functioned together in a marvelously coordinated effort. There was real harmony and fellowship in the networking that the Lord had put together: *fellow* servant, *fellow* prisoner, *fellow* workers. Paul was the apostle called specially by God and given a high place in the divine scheme of things, but as far as Paul was concerned, he was on the same level as all of these people with whom he was in fellowship in the work of the gospel.

May I say that one of the strongest witnesses that we as a church family can have to our community is for us to be of one accord, to be one in Christ. That doesn't mean that we don't have differences. That doesn't mean that we all will see things exactly the same way. It doesn't mean uniformity—but it does mean that there will be mutual love and respect. It means that we will function as the body of Christ and complement one another as we serve together. The people before us were scattered by hundreds of miles and each had a unique role to fill and a different place in which to serve Christ, but they had a strong bond.

Variety

There was racial variety: Jew and Gentile. I love it when I can shake the hand of a black brother after a service or dedicate a little native baby. I love it when I see colored skins, when I see people of a variety of ethnic and racial backgrounds in the church. We are an international church, a church that seeks, by the grace of God, to put our arms around the whole world. When we cease being that we will cease being a New Testament church.

There was social variety: free men and slave. There was vocational variety: an apostle, pastors, missionary evangelists, a physician and a slave. In Roman culture a slave was as low as you could go—and yet Paul refers to this slave as a beloved brother. He had no social status in Rome but he was a part of the family of God, the household of faith. He was a child of the King.

Aren't you glad for variety? I love variety. We need shepherds, we need sheep, we need teachers, we need people to be taught, we need helpers, we need people who need help, we need givers, we need people to whom we give help. We have great variety within the church, and this is God's gift to us. Let us embrace it as such.

Sensitivity

In their service there was also sensitivity. "Onesimus, our faithful and dear brother, who is one of you" (4:9). Paul sent

Onesimus, the runaway slave, back to Rome with Tychicus, who carried the letter. He was coming back to his hometown and into church for the first time. He had been an outsider. He was a runaway slave. He had disgraced his owner. God in His grace brought him in touch with Paul in Rome and Paul led him to Christ, and now he was an insider and Paul was sending him home a "dear brother." Isn't that a sensitive thing? Paul never said, "I am sending this runaway slave back. He was unprofitable. He is not a very good person, you know. He really failed. Anyway, he is coming." No. Onesimus was called a "faithful and dear brother." The grace of God had changed things.

He mentioned Mark. He didn't say, "John Mark, the missionary casualty, is coming to you—welcome him." He could have, because John Mark *was* a missionary casualty. He had gone with Paul and Barnabas on the first missionary journey and dropped out and went home. But Paul didn't say anything about that; he said, "Welcome him" (4:10). God used John Mark in a marvelous way as the writer of the second Gospel. He was restored. He had made a mistake, yes; there was failure in his past, yes; but that was over. He is now someone to be welcomed by the church at Colosse.

Are we sensitive about how we say things to each other and what we say about each other? Real servants are focused on the needs of people and real servants never put people down. A real servant lifts people up. He makes them feel better. He serves their needs. He says, "I am here for you." Are we sensitive? Some of you may need to write a little thank you note to someone. Others may need to express love for someone. And there is always need for us to say to people we have hurt, "I am sorry."

Spirituality

We throw this word "spirituality" around a lot. It is spiritually minded people who are committed to the spiritual needs and welfare of other people. These people in our chapter were spiritually minded. Not a word about personal needs is given here. Not a word about personal desires, personal ambitions, personal accomplishments.

Paul said in 4:8: "I am sending him [Tychicus] to you for the express purpose that you may know about our circumstances and that he may encourage your hearts." That's Paul. He needed comfort; he needed help—he was in prison! But he was sending Tychicus to Colosse to comfort them. In 4:11, Paul said that his fellow workers had proved to be a comfort and blessing to him. Then he said in 4:12-13: "Epaphras, who is one of you and a servant of Christ Jesus, sends greetings. He is always wrestling in prayer for you, that you may stand firm in all the will of God, mature and fully assured. I vouch for him that he is working hard for you and for those at Laodicea and Hierapolis." Epaphras was their pastor, one of them, the man who founded the church. Paul said, "He is always wrestling in prayer for you. . . . He is working hard for you" (4:12-13). That is what spiritual ministry is all about. That is what serving people is all about.

Accountability

Finally, in their service there was accountability. One of the men, Archippus, who was a member of the church in Colosse, had evidently been called into the ministry. That is, he had been ordained by God and recognized by the church as one called to preach and teach the word of God. Notice what he said to this man: "See to it that you complete the work you have received in the Lord" (4:17). Keep your ordination vows. Be true to Christ who called you to preach His gospel. Fulfill the will of God. Do what you have been called to do. Paul was calling him to accountability. He wasn't scolding him; he was just saying, "I know God has called you. Now do what He has called to you to do. Be what He has called you to be."

All of us pastors need accountability. We need to be accountable to our Boards. We need to be accountable to other ministers. We certainly need to be accountable to our wives and families. It is so important that we be accountable and that we complete the work assigned to us.

Paul said it eloquently before the Ephesian elders in Acts 20:24: "However, I consider my life worth nothing to me, if only I may finish the race and complete the task the Lord Jesus has given me."

And so this marvelous epistle on the supremacy and sufficiency of Christ ends and on a very practical note. It is obvious that when Christ is supreme in our lives, our deepest desire will be to serve Him by serving others. We cannot call Him Lord and Master and then fail to do what He has called us to do.

Questions for Reflection or Discussion

1. In our study we speak about "outsiders" and "insiders." How would you define these?

2. What is our first responsibility in our service to "outsiders"? Give details.

3. How did the Lord give Paul "openings" in a "closed" environment?

4. Give six ways believers can be "wise" in the way we act and witness before "outsiders."

5. Discuss "salty" and gracious words in the speech of believers. Who is the prime example?

6. List some of the words to describe Paul's colleagues in the ministry.

7. Give the five words that describe and define true service. Discuss each one.

Endnote

1. Charles Erdman, *An Exposition: The Epistle of Colossians and Philemon* (Philadelphia: Westminster Press, 1933), p. 101.

Philemon

12

Philemon

Philemon 1-25

Paul, a prisoner of Christ Jesus, and Timothy our brother,

To Philemon our dear friend and fellow worker, to Apphia our sister, to Archippus our fellow soldier and to the church that meets in your home:

Grace to you and peace from God our Father and the Lord Jesus Christ.

I always thank my God as I remember you in my prayers, because I hear about your faith in the Lord Jesus and your love for all the saints. I pray that you may be active in sharing your faith, so that you will have a full understanding of every good thing we have in Christ. Your love has given me great joy and encouragement, because you, brother, have refreshed the hearts of the saints.

Therefore, although in Christ I could be bold and order you to do what you ought to do, yet I appeal to you on the basis of love. I then, as Paul—an old man and now also a prisoner of Christ Jesus—I appeal to you for my son Onesimus, who became my son while I was in chains. Formerly he was useless to you, but now he has become useful both to you and to me.

I am sending him—who is my very heart—back to you. I would have liked to keep him with me so that he could take your place in helping me while I am in chains for the gospel. But I did not want to do anything without your consent, so that any favor you do will be spontaneous and not forced. Perhaps the reason he was separated from you for a little while was that you might have him back for good—no longer as a slave, but better than a slave, as a dear brother. He is very dear to me but even dearer to you, both as a man and as a brother in the Lord.

So if you consider me a partner, welcome him as you would welcome me. If he has done you any wrong or owes you anything, charge it to me. I, Paul, am writing this with my own hand. I will pay it back—not to mention that you owe me your very self. I do wish, brother, that I may have some benefit from you in the Lord; refresh my heart in Christ. Confident of your obedience, I write to you, knowing that you will do even more than I ask.

And one thing more: Prepare a guest room for me, because I hope to be restored to you in answer to your prayers.

Epaphras, my fellow prisoner in Christ Jesus, sends you greetings. And so do Mark, Aristarchus, Demas and Luke, my fellow workers.

The grace of the Lord Jesus Christ be with your spirit.

We are considering, in this concluding chapter, the briefest of all Paul's epistles—the epistle to Philemon. But, as in many instances, the size of the letter does not tell its true value. Indeed we have at least three large lessons in this little letter, treasures of truth in miniature:

1. The Providence of Life
2. The Practice of Love
3. The Principles of Law.

The Providence of Life

Providence is that constant and perfect care by Almighty God by which He guarantees that all circumstances and events work out for good for those who trust Him. Providence is always related to people; therefore, we must identify the people who are involved in the drama that this letter unfolds.

- *Paul*, of course, is the author and is writing from a Roman prison cell.

- *Philemon* is a wealthy slave owner from Colosse. The church meets in his home.

- *Apphia* is Philemon's wife.

- *Archippus* is probably Philemon's son and a member of the Colossian assembly.

- *Onesimus* is a slave owned by Philemon who has run away to Rome. His name means "profitable." Through contact with Paul, he has come to Christ.

- *Tychicus* is the courier of both the Colossian epistle and this letter to Philemon. He is also escorting Onesimus back home (Colossians 4:7-9).

Placement and providence

Paul viewed his placement in the prison in Rome as having a definite and vital connection with the Lord Jesus Christ. He identifies himself in the salutation in Philemon 1 as "a prisoner of Christ Jesus." This interesting expression suggests *relationship*. It was because of his relationship with the Lord Jesus that he was in prison in the first place. He was there suffering humiliation and deprivation because he belonged to God's Son, whom Rome hated. Paul considered it a badge of honor to identify himself with Jesus.

His placement in the prison cell also suggests *Lordship*. He was the prisoner of the Lord, not of Rome or Caesar or the devil or forces beyond God's control. He believed that Jesus Christ was in control of his affairs and that he was where he was not by accident but by appointment—divine appointment.

Joseph Parker speaks eloquently regarding this great truth:

But Paul never consented to live within the literal meaning of the word "prison." To that term he added others, and thus he glorified it. It is not "Paul, a prisoner," it is "Paul, a prisoner of Jesus Christ"—where is the gaol now? "My fellow-prisoner in Jesus Christ"; "I Paul, the prisoner of the Lord." How much richer we might be, if we drew more heavily upon the bank of the riches of Christ! There would be those who called themselves mere prisoners; they saw nothing but the prison walls, they felt nothing but the prison chains, they spoke of nothing but the prison diet and deprivation of companionship and many of the advantages of civilization. Paul never talked in a whining tone. He enlarged the gaol by taking Christ into it, and when they were both together, though in prison, they were in heaven. The Apostle Paul always looked beyond the gaoler; he said to him in effect, You are but an instrument; you carry the keys, and yet you are only a key yourself; you do not know what you are doing; I bear you no resentment or animosity, you are in the hands of the king.[1]

Fellowship was also an essential element in Paul's prison experience. He was not only a prisoner *of* Christ Jesus, he was also a prisoner *in* Christ Jesus (23). The Lord not only put Paul in prison, He also put Paul in Himself. His location was a Roman prison but his position was in the Lord Jesus . . . Himself! I can deal with my location, as difficult as it may be, if I am certain of my spiritual position. There is no question that Paul drew from the enormous strength and grace that came from being in the Lord. The drab cell was transformed by the glorious presence of the Lord Jesus.

Prayer and providence

When the Lord in His all-wise providence places us in tight places, difficult places or even impossible places, He often teaches us there how to pray. Prison shut Paul in but it didn't shut him up! Bars hindered his horizontal movement but it couldn't stop his vertical movement. He was really shut up to faith and God and prayer as never before. He said to Philemon, "I remember you in my prayers" (4). He could not be with Philemon in person to minister to him, but he could and did hold him up to the throne of grace in intercession. When he couldn't enjoy a prophetic ministry to him, he could enter into a priestly ministry for him. Both are equally important. The Lord has His own ways of bringing balance into our lives.

Paul's imprisonment not only stimulated his prayer life, it also stimulated prayer in the lives of the believers who knew his situation. He was confident that their prayers would make a definite difference in his situation. At verse 22 he said, "I hope to be restored to you in *answer to your prayers*" (emphasis added). So the prisoner prays and is prayed for.

Providence does not relieve us of prayer responsibility. We are not fatalists. Even though he was in prison by divine appointment, Paul wasn't "locked in" to that situation without any other recourse. He knew that the Lord would release him and he knew that prayer was the key.

Cecil has said, "Duties are ours; events are God's." We must leave the events with Him but our duty is to pray.[2]

South, with clear insight speaks to this matter.

> To make our reliance upon providence both pious and rational, we should prepare all things with the same care, diligence, and activity, as if there were no such thing as providence for us to depend upon; and then, when we have done all this, we should as wholly and

humbly rely upon it, as if we had made no preparation at all.[3]

Productivity and providence

We can view obstacles and problems in one of two ways: something to stop us, or something to stimulate us. Some people view difficulties as a providential excuse for not being productive. Others, such as Paul, view difficulties as providential opportunities to be productive—maybe not in the way we had wished, but an opportunity nonetheless.

Was Paul productive in prison? Consider the following:

1. *He prayed.* He drew upon heaven's resources in a new and vital way. Check out his prison epistles—Ephesians, Philippians, Colossians, Second Timothy and, of course, Philemon—and you will find some of the great prayers of the Bible.
2. *He wrote letters.* Some of the deepest and most doctrinally rich of all his writings came out of his prison experiences.
3. *He continued witnessing.* Onesimus was some of his evangelistic fruit. He told the Philippians that even though he was fettered, the gospel was furthered or advanced. Through some of the guard converts, the Word of God had actually reached into Caesar's household (Philippians 1:12-14; 4:22).

What a joy it must have been for Paul to refer to Onesimus as "my son" and to Philemon as "dear brother." Great productivity for a man with a chain on his wrist!

Another great theme for this little letter is . . .

The Practice of Love

How love is experienced

We learn something about how love is experienced in Philemon 5 where Paul said, "I hear about your faith in the Lord Jesus and your love for all the saints." He said the very same thing to the Colossian congregation (Colossians 1:4). Faith brings us into a relationship with Jesus Christ and that relationship is indeed love experienced. We could look at it in the following way:

FAITH	**LOVE**
Vertical	Horizontal
Relationship established	Fellowship experienced
Focused on the Savior	Focused on the saints
Finds the source	Finds the object
The root	The fruit

Paul said in Galatians 5:6: "The only thing that counts is faith expressing itself through love."

In Christ we have: the Sacrifice of Love (John 15:13); the Source of Love (Ephesians 3:17-19); and the Spirit of Love (Romans 5:5). It is obvious, therefore, that we can never really know the love of God until we know the Son of His love, the Lord Jesus Christ.

How love is expressed

Paul said, "I hear about . . . your love for all the saints" (Philemon 5). True love is always heard about. People can see it expressed and they talk about it. We must remember that this kind of love is a verb—always active, always at work. We cannot always define it, but we can always see in it action.

Philemon expressed his love by "refresh[ing] the hearts of the saints" (7). Undoubtedly he used the material assets at his disposal to help the people in the congregation of Colosse. The word translated "refresh" is *annpauo* and has in it both the idea of a person's back and causing to cease. The thought is that by love Philemon had lifted burdens from the backs of the saints whom he knew. Paul instructed us in Galatians 6:2 to "carry each other's burdens, and in this way you will fulfill the law of Christ."

All of us can see people all around us with burdens. But we must do more than just see their burdens. Seeing love expressed by Philemon brought joy and encouragement to Paul in prison. Not only were the saints blessed in Colosse, but Paul was blessed in Rome! Love expressed always abounds and rebounds in many ways. Little did Philemon realize when he loved the believers near him that that love would reach all the way into a dark prison cell in Rome and bring joy and consolation to the great apostle.

How love is entreated

In the passage before us we learn about how love is entreated. When Paul began to appeal to Philemon for Onesimus' reinstatement and restoration, he said, "Therefore, although in Christ I could be bold and order you to do what you ought to do, yet I appeal to you on the *basis of love*" (Philemon 8-9, emphasis mine).

Paul was making an appeal for Onesimus, but he was basing that request on love, not apostolic muscle. He is entreating Philemon *by* love but he also is entreating Philemon *to* love—to love Onesimus and receive him back not as a runaway slave but as a dear brother (16). Paul knew that Philemon had already demonstrated that he was a man of love, so this request is not at all presumptuous.

All of this is done with some very subtle yet very real qualities of love in Paul.

1. Because of love, Paul didn't abuse his apostolic authority (8-9). Love never throws its weight around or forces people to do things without their free consent.

2. Because of love, Paul appealed to the most noble and highest character qualities in Philemon (10-14).

3. Because of love, Paul passed by personal needs—needs which Onesimus could have met—in order to put Philemon's needs first (11-14).

4. Because of love, Paul had high expectations of Philemon. He said, "knowing that you will do even more than I ask" (21). Love "always trusts, always hopes" (1 Corinthians 13:7).

When we are habitually doubtful of others and do not believe the best about them, it is often because we really do not love them. Love is perpetually optimistic.

The final great important theme for Philemon is . . .

The Principles of Law

Certainly, this brief portion of God's inspired Word does not give us a technical or structural statement about law, but we find law all the way through. We see various elements of law all through the fabric of this very practical epistle.

Moral law

Paul alludes to moral law in Philemon 18: "If he has done you any wrong or owes you anything, charge it to me." Obviously, there must be some way to determine what is right or wrong. If we say something is wrong, there must be some standard of conduct which has not been reached. The person has violated a law.

This raises the question of right and wrong. In an age of relativism, when many reject all absolutes in matters of morals and ethics, can we really know what is right and wrong? The answer, of course, is yes. Our Creator has, by right, His absolute sovereignty, given us moral law. This has come in two forms: 1. the Decalogue or ten commandments; 2. natural law or the law written on the heart (Romans 2:14-15)

Through Moses, the Lord gave us the ten commandments as His written statement to all the sons of men regarding right and wrong. Some in our day, through an exaggerated emphasis on grace, would have us think that the law was not a good thing. You would almost think that they believe God made a mistake. But Paul said that the law is holy, and the commandment is holy, righteous and good. He also said that in his inner being he delighted in God's law (7:12, 22).

Why was it given, then, and why is it good? The ten commandments

1. Express the holy character of God (Psalm 119:137-138).

2. Reveal man's sinfulness and guilt (Romans 3:19-20).

3. Bring us to Christ (Galatians 3:24).

4. Provide an objective statement to all men in all ages of God's absolute standard of righteousness (Ephesians 4:25-5:8).

   (Five of the commandments are repeated in this passage with New Testament applications. And this in an epistle that is rich in the teaching of grace!)

Even apart from the law inscribed in stone, all people have another law written in their hearts. We call this natural law, and it is universally experienced. All people know in their hearts that certain things are right and other things are wrong. God is just as much the author of this moral consciousness as He is the law written by Moses.

John Calvin said, "Distinction between virtuous and vicious actions has been engraven in the heart of every man by God."[4] Many others have made the same observation. C.S. Lewis offers the thought that the whole basis for human quarreling is trying to show that another person is wrong. There obviously would be no point in trying to do this if there were no understanding of what right and wrong are.[5]

Ecclesiastical law

Paul suggests this law in Philemon 8-9. Because of his apostolic authority, Paul could have commanded Philemon to receive Onesimus back. He did not do that because it would have been an abuse of that authority. He didn't order Philemon on the basis of his position but rather appealed to him on the basis of love.

The apostle also did not project ecclesiastical strength but rather spoke from a place of personal weakness. He speaks of himself as an "old man" and a "prisoner of Christ Jesus." There are many practical lessons here for any who have leadership positions in the church. Certainly our authority in the church is always exercised in love and with the full benefit of God's flock always before us. We never insist on our rights but gladly accept our responsibility.

Civil law

Paul recognizes civil law or the law of the Roman Empire all the way through this letter. Under that law, Philemon really did own Onesimus. He was his property and had no rights at all. Remember that there were 60 million slaves under the heel of imperial Rome at that time. With that many, a possible rebellion was always a threat and Rome treated insubordinate slaves with immediate execution. Dr. William Barclay tells us that a runaway slave could expect at the very best to be branded on his forehead with a red-hot iron, with the letter F standing for "fugitive."[6]

Paul certainly wanted to honor the law of the land, and yet he wanted to do the Christian thing for both Philemon and Onesimus. The only time the Bible teaches civil disobedience in when the state requires us to violate the moral law of God. Then, as Peters says so eloquently, "We must obey God rather than men!" (Acts 5:29).

Spiritual law

Spiritual law is called different things in the New Testament:

1. The law of Christ—"Carry each other's burdens" (Galatians 6:2).

2. The royal law—"Love your neighbor as yourself" (James 2:8).

3. The new commandment—"Love one another. As I have loved you, so you must love one another" (John 13:34).

4. It is called the law of the Spirit of life—"Through Christ Jesus the law of the Spirit of life has set me free from the law of sin and death" (Romans 8:2).

Please see how this law worked in Paul's life as he dealt with the profoundly delicate problem between Onesimus and Philemon.

POSTURE of this law

Paul called himself a prisoner of Christ and never stands on the merits of his position. He honored Philemon's legal rights and position. We dealt with this earlier, but again we underline the fact that when we are controlled by the law of Christ's love, we take the low place of serving others rather than ordering them or seeking to control them.

The apostle even identified with the runaway and law-breaking slave and implored Philemon to welcome him home even as he would welcome Paul (Philemon 17).

POSITIVENESS *of this law*

Everything that Paul says about both Philemon and Onesimus is positive. The spiritual law is Christ will always give us love for people and seek constructive and positive ways of blessing them. Paul calls Philemon a "dear friend and fellow worker" (1). He thanks God for him and prays for him (4). He commends him for his love and the way he has refreshed the saints (7). He is very pleased that Philemon can now receive Onesimus back as a dear "brother in the Lord" (16). Paul is also very confident that Philemon will refresh his heart and do even more than he has requested (20-21).

Paul, in his appeal for Onesimus, calls him "my son" (10) and one who is now useful to both Philemon and himself (11). Onesimus is no longer a slave. He is better than a slave—he is a dear "brother in the Lord" (16). When the royal law is applied, all artificial differences are removed and only our spiritual oneness in the family of God is recognized.

PRACTICALITY *of this law*

When we are under the control of the spiritual law of Christ, we will always do practical things, and we will always go beyond the civil law. Paul did many things because of love's constraints, as we have already seen. But Paul did one additional thing in his desire to be involved in Onesimus' restoration to Philemon.

His prayers and his tender and extremely sensitive letter would have probably accomplished a healed relationship between the master and his slave, but Paul goes beyond this and offers to pay for any debt that Onesimus has toward Philemon:

"charge it to me" or as the NKJV has it, "put that on my account" (18).

True Christianity—spiritual living—isn't just talking about religious concepts and going through religious motions. It is far more practical. It is paying bills and taking responsibilities for others who cannot help themselves. It is moving out of our comfort zone and becoming liable and vulnerable for people who don't count for much in the eyes of the world.

We can't say for sure how all of this turned out. But I am confident that grace triumphed and that love won the day. I believe that Onesimus was received back by his brother Philemon and became a profitable servant and a loyal member of the church in Colosse. And I believe that Paul occupied the guest room in answer to prayer and that he—the apostle—and the master and slave all embraced in the love of Christ.

Questions for Reflection or Discussion

1. How would you support from the epistle that Paul was in the prison cell by divine appointment?
2. Identify Philemon and Onesimus and their relationship to each other. What was the problem between them?
3. Was Paul productive in prison? Explain how.
4. What was Paul's basis for appealing to Philemon for Onesimus' restoration?
5. What were some of the ways Paul expressed love to Philemon?
6. What are the four kinds of law that are touched upon in this letter?
7. Does the law of Moses have any relevance today?
8. Give three of the names for the spiritual law that we find in Scripture. Is this law operating in your life?

Endnotes

1. Joseph Parker, *The People's Bible* (Grand Rapids, MI: Baker Book House, 1978), p. 165.
2. *The New Dictionary of Thoughts* (New York: Standard Book Co., 1936), p. 511.
3. Ibid., p. 512.
4. John Calvin, quoted in *Day Brighteners* (Minneapolis, MN: Northwestern Products, n.d.), n.p.
5. C.S. Lewis, *Mere Christianity* (New York: The MacMillan Co., 1958), pp. 3-4.
6. William Barclay, *Timothy, Titus, and Philemon,* Daily Bible Series (Toronto, ON: Welch Co., 1956), p. 270.

Bibliography

Barclay, William. *The Letters to the Philippians, Colossians, and Thessalonians.* Daily Bible Studies. Toronto, ON: Welch Co., 1956 (Reprinted 1984).

Barclay, William. *Timothy, Titus, and Philemon.* Daily Bible Studies. Toronto, ON: Welch Co., 1956 (Reprinted 1984).

Carson, H.M. *Colossians and Philemon.* Tyndale New Testament Commentaries. Leicester, England: InterVarsity Press, 1960 (Reprinted 1984).

Chapman, J. Wilbur. "Our Great Saviour," *Hymns of the Christian Life.* Camp Hill, PA: Christian Publications, 1978.

Copeland, Lewis and Lamm, Lawrence W. *The World's Great Speeches.* New York: D.D. Hodder and Stoughton, 1898.

Erdman, Charles R. *An Exposition: The Epistle of Paul to the Colossians and Philemon.* Philadelphia: Westminster Press, 1933.

Lenski, R.C.H. *The Interpretation of Colossians.* Minneapolis, MN: Augsburg Publishing House, 1937.

Moule, H.C.G. *Colossians Studies.* New York: D.D. Hodder and Stoughton, 1898.

New Dictionary of Thoughts. New York: Standard Book Co., 1936.

Parker, Joseph. *The People's Bible.* Grand Rapids, MI: Baker Book House, 1978.

Robertson, A.T. *Paul and the Intellectuals.* Nashville, TN: Broadman Press, 1956 (Revised 1959).

Simpson, A.B. "Christ in Me," *Hymns of the Christian Life*. Camp Hill, PA: Christian Publications, 1978.

Simpson, A.B. *Himself*. Camp Hill, PA: Christian Publications, 1991.

Stott, John R.W. *Between Two Worlds*. Grand Rapids, MI: Eerdmans, 1982.

Sturtz, Richard. *Studies in Colossians*. Chicago: Moody Press, 1955.

Wuest, *Word Studies in the Greek New Testament*. Grand Rapids, MI: Eerdmans, 1953.

Bibles

Life Application Bible (Living Bible). Wheaton, IL: Tyndale, 1988.

The Ryrie Study Bible (KJV). Chicago: Moody Press, 1976.

The Holy Bible (NIV). Grand Rapids, MI: Zondervan, 1984.

The Open Bible (NKJV). New York: Thomas Nelson, Inc., 1985.

The Holy Bible (KJV). Mt. Holly, NJ: Franklin Electronic Publishers Inc., 1989-93.